# THE IDEA OF
# A SOCIAL SCIENCE

# STUDIES IN
# PHILOSOPHICAL PSYCHOLOGY

*Edited by*
## R. F. HOLLAND

# THE IDEA OF
# A SOCIAL SCIENCE

and its Relation to Philosophy

*by*

PETER WINCH

LONDON AND HENLEY

ROUTLEDGE & KEGAN PAUL

NEW YORK: HUMANITIES PRESS

*First published in Great Britain 1958*
*by Routledge & Kegan Paul Ltd*
*39 Store Street, London WC1E 2DD and*
*Reading Road, Henley-on-Thames, Oxon. RG9 1EN*

*Second impression 1960*
*Third impression (with some corrections) 1963*
*Fourth impression 1965*
*Fifth impression 1967*
*Sixth impression 1970*
*Seventh impression 1971*
*Eighth impression 1973*
*Ninth impression 1976*

*Printed in Great Britain by*
*Redwood Burn Limited*
*Trowbridge & Esher*

*ISBN 0 7100 3835 6 (c)*
*ISBN 0 7100 6804 2 (p)*

*Denn wenn es schon wahr ist, dass moralische Handlungen, sie mögen zu noch so verschiednen Zeiten, bey noch so verschiednen Völkern vorkommen, in sich betrachtet immer die nehmlichen bleiben: so haben doch darum die nehmlichen Handlungen nicht immer die nehmlichen Benennungen, und es ist ungerecht, irgend einer eine andere Benennung zu geben, als die, welche sie zu ihren Zeiten, und bey ihrem Volk zu haben pflegte.*

(It may indeed be true that moral actions are always the same in themselves, however different may be the times and however different the societies in which they occur; but still, the same actions do not always have the same names, and it is unjust to give any action a different name from that which it used to bear in its own times and amongst its own people.)

(GOTTHOLD EPHRAIM LESSING: *Anti-Goeze*).

# CONTENTS

CONTENTS

———————◆———————

# CHAPTER ONE

# PHILOSOPHICAL BEARINGS

## 1. *Aims and Strategy*

THAT the social sciences are in their infancy has come to be a platitude amongst writers of textbooks on the subject. They will argue that this is because the social sciences have been slow to emulate the natural sciences and emancipate themselves from the dead hand of philosophy; that there was a time when there was no clear distinction between philosophy and natural science; but that owing to the transformation of this state of affairs round about the seventeenth century natural science has made great bounds ever since. But, we are told, this revolution has not yet taken place in the social sciences, or at least it is only now in process of taking place. Perhaps social science has not yet found its Newton but the conditions are being created in which such a genius could arise. But above all, it is urged, we must follow the methods of natural science rather than those of philosophy if we are to make any significant progress.

I propose, in this monograph, to attack such a conception of the relation between the social studies, philosophy and the natural sciences. But it should not be assumed on that account that what I have to say

1

must be ranked with those reactionary anti-scientific movements, aiming to put the clock back, which have appeared and flourished in certain quarters since science began. My only aim is to make sure that the clock is telling the right time, whatever it may prove to be. Philosophy, for reasons which may be made more apparent subsequently, has no business to be anti-scientific: if it tries to be so it will succeed only in making itself look ridiculous. Such attacks are as distasteful and undignified as they are useless and unphilosophical. But equally, and for the same reasons, philosophy must be on its guard against the extra-scientific *pretensions* of science. Since science is one of the chief shibboleths of the present age this is bound to make the philosopher unpopular; he is likely to meet a similar reaction to that met by someone who criticizes the monarchy. But the day when philosophy becomes a popular subject is the day for the philosopher to consider where he took the wrong turning.

I said that my aim was to attack a current conception of the relations between philosophy and the social studies. Since that conception involves two terms, what may appear to some a disproportionately large portion of this book must be devoted to discussing matters whose bearing on the nature of the social studies is not immediately evident. The view I wish to commend presupposes a certain conception of philosophy, a conception which many will think as heretical as my conception of social science itself. So, however irrelevant it may at first appear, a discussion of the nature of philosophy is an *essential* part of the argument of this book. This opening chapter, then, cannot safely be skipped as a tiresome and time-wasting preliminary.

This may be more convincing if I briefly outline the general strategy of the book. It will consist of a war on two fronts: first, a criticism of some prevalent contemporary ideas about the nature of philosophy; second, a criticism of some prevalent contemporary ideas about the nature of the social studies. The main tactics will be a pincer movement: the same point will be reached by arguing from opposite directions. To complete the military analogy before it gets out of hand, my main war aim will be to demonstrate that the two apparently diverse fronts on which the war is being waged are not in reality diverse at all; that to be clear about the nature of philosophy and to be clear about the nature of the social studies amount to the same thing. For any worthwhile study of society must be philosophical in character and any worthwhile philosophy must be concerned with the nature of human society.

## 2. *The Underlabourer Conception of Philosophy*

I will call the conception of philosophy which I want to criticize the 'underlabourer conception', in honour of one of its presiding geniuses, John Locke. The following passage from the Epistle to the Reader which prefaces Locke's *Essay Concerning Human Understanding*, is often quoted with approval by supporters of the underlabourer conception.

The commonwealth of learning is not at this time without master-builders, whose mighty designs, in

advancing the sciences, will leave lasting monuments to
the admiration of posterity: but everyone must not hope
to be a Boyle or a Sydenham; and in an age that produces
such masters as the great Huygenius and the incomparable
Mr. Newton, with some others of that strain, it is ambition
enough to be employed as an under-labourer in clearing
the ground a little, and removing some of the rubbish that
lies in the way to knowledge.

Locke's view is echoed in A. J. Ayer's distinction
between the 'pontiffs' and the 'journeymen' of
philosophy; it is translated into the idiom of much
modern philosophical discussion by A. G. N. Flew, in
his introduction to *Logic and Language* (First Series);
and it has many points of contact with Gilbert Ryle's
conception of philosophy as 'informal logic' (Cf.
Gilbert Ryle: *Dilemmas*, Cambridge).

I will try to isolate some of the outstanding features
of this view which are most relevant for my present
purpose. First, there is the idea that 'it is by its methods rather than its subject-matter that philosophy is
to be distinguished from other arts or sciences' (3).
That obviously follows from the underlabourer
conception; for according to it philosophy cannot
contribute any positive understanding of the world on
its own account: it has the purely negative role of
removing impediments to the advance of our understanding. The motive force for that advance must be
sought in methods quite different from anything to be
found in philosophy; it must be found, that is, in
science. On this view philosophy is parasitic on other
disciplines; it has no problems of its own but is a
technique for solving problems thrown up in the
course of non-philosophical investigations.

The modern conception of what constitutes the 'rubbish that lies in the way to knowledge' is very similar to Locke's own: philosophy is concerned with eliminating linguistic confusions. So the picture we are presented with is something like this. Genuine new knowledge is acquired by scientists by experimental and observational methods. Language is a tool which is indispensible to this process; like any other tool language can develop defects, and those which are peculiar to it are logical contradictions, often conceived on the analogy of mechanical faults in material tools. Just as other sorts of tool need a specialist mechanic to maintain them in good order, so with language. Whereas a garage mechanic is concerned with removing such things as blockages in carburettors, a philosopher removes contradictions from realms of discourse.

I turn now to a further, connected, implication of the underlabourer conception. If the problems of philosophy come to it from without, it becomes necessary to give some special account of the role of metaphysics and epistemology within philosophy. For though it may be plausible to say that the problems of the philosophy of science, the philosophy of religion, the philosophy of art, and so on, are set *for* philosophy by science, religion, art, etc., it is not at all obvious what sets the problems for metaphysics and epistemology. If we say that these disciplines are autonomous with regard to their problems, then of course the underlabourer conception collapses as an exhaustive account of the nature of philosophy. Some writers have suggested that metaphysics and epistemology are just the philosophies of science and of psychology respectively in disguise, but I have never seen this view defended in any detail and it is certainly not *prima facie* plausible to anyone who is at all familiar with the history of these subjects. Others again have said that metaphysical and epistemological discussions are an entirely spurious form of activity and do not belong to any respectable discipline at all. But they treat of questions which have a habit of recurring and such a cavalier attitude soon begins to ring somewhat hollow. It is in fact a good deal less popular than once it was.

Another widely held view is that championed, for instance, by Peter Laslett in his editorial introduction to *Philosophy, Politics and Society* (13). According to this view, the preoccupation with epistemological questions, which has for some time characterized philosophical discussion in this country, is to be construed as a temporary phase, as a period of examining and improving the *tools* of philosophy, rather than as the very stuff of philosophy itself. The idea is that, when this work of re-tooling has been done, it is the duty of the philosopher to return to his more important task—that of clarifying the concepts which belong to other, non-philosophical disciplines.

In the first place this interpretation is unhistorical, since epistemological questions have always been central to serious philosophical work, and it is difficult to see how this could be otherwise. More importantly, Laslett's view involves a reversal of the true order of priority within philosophy: epistemological discussion is represented as important only in so far as it serves a further end, namely to advance the treatment of questions in the philosophies of science, art, politics, etc. I want to argue, on the contrary, that the philosophies of science, art, politics, etc.— subjects which I will call the 'peripheral' philosophical disciplines —lose their philosophical character if unrelated to epistemology and metaphysics. But before I can show this in detail, I must first attempt to examine the philosophical foundations of the underlabourer conception of philosophy.

### 3.  *Philosophy and Science*

That conception is in large part a reaction against the 'master-scientist' view of the philosopher, according to which philosophy is in direct competition with science and aims at constructing or refuting scientific theories by purely *a priori* reasoning. This is an idea which is justly ridiculed; the absurdities to which it may lead are amply illustrated in Hegel's amateur pseudo-scientific speculations. Its philosophical refutation was provided by Hume:

> If we would satisfy ourselves . . . concerning the nature of that evidence, which assures us of matters of fact, we must enquire how we arrive at the knowledge of cause and effect. I shall venture to affirm, as a general proposition, which admits of no exception, that the knowledge of this relation is not, in any instance, attained by reasonings *a priori;* but arises entirely from experience, when we find that any particular objects are constantly conjoined with each other. Let an object be presented to a man of never so strong natural reason and abilities; if that object be entirely new to him, he will not be able, by the most accurate examination of its sensible qualities, to discover any of its causes or effects. (12: Section IV, Part I.)

Now this is admirable as a critique of *a priori* pseudo-science. But the argument has also frequently been misapplied in order to attack *a priori* philosophizing of a sort which is quite legitimate. The argument runs as follows : new discoveries about real matters of fact can only be established by experimental methods; no purely *a priori* process of thinking is sufficient for this. But since it is science which uses experimental methods, while philosophy is purely *a priori*, it follows that the investigation of reality must be left to science. On the other hand, philosophy has traditionally claimed, at least in large part, to consist in the investigation of the nature of reality; either, therefore, traditional philosophy was attempting to do something which its methods of investigation could never possibly achieve, and must be abandoned; or else it was mistaken about its own nature, and the purport of its investigations must be drastically reinterpreted.

Now the argument on which this dilemma is based is fallacious: it contains an undistributed middle term. The phrase 'the investigation of the nature of reality' is ambiguous, and whereas Hume's argument applies perfectly well to what that phrase conveys when applied to *scientific* investigation, it is a mere *ignoratio elenchi* as applied to *philosophy*. The difference between the respective aims of the scientist and the philosopher might be expressed as follows. Whereas the scientist investigates the nature, causes and effects of *particular* real things and processes, the philosopher is concerned with the nature of reality as such and in general. Burnet puts the point very well in his book on *Greek Philosophy* when he points out (on pages 11 and 12) that the sense in which the philosopher asks

'What is real?' involves the problem of man's relation to reality, which takes us beyond pure science. 'We have to ask whether the mind of man can have any contact with reality at all, and, if it can, what difference this will make to his life'. Now to think that this question of Burnet's could be settled by experimental methods involves just as serious a mistake as to think that philosophy, with its *a priori* methods of reasoning, could possibly compete with experimental science on its own ground. For it is not an empirical question at all, but a *conceptual* one. It has to do with the *force of the concept* of reality. An appeal to the results of an experiment would necessarily beg the important question, since the philosopher would be bound to ask by what token those results themselves are accepted as 'reality'. Of course, this simply exasperates the experimental scientist—rightly so, from the point of view of his own aims and interests. But the force of the philosophical question cannot be grasped in terms of the preconceptions of experimental science. It cannot be answered by generalizing from particular instances since a particular answer to the philosophical question is already implied in the acceptance of those instances as 'real'.

The whole issue was symbolically dramatized on a celebrated occasion in 1939 when Professor G. E. Moore gave a lecture to the British Academy entitled 'Proof of an External World'. Moore's 'proof' ran roughly as follows. He held up each of his hands in succession, saying 'Here is one hand and here is another; therefore at least two external objects exist; therefore an external world exists'. In arguing thus Moore seemed to be treating the question 'Does an external world exist?' as similar in form to the question 'Do animals with a single horn growing out of their snout exist?' This of course would be conclusively settled by the production of two rhinoceri. But the bearing of Moore's argument on the philosophical question of the existence of an external world is not as simple as the bearing of the production of two rhinoceri on the other question. For, of course, philosophical doubt about the existence of an external world covers the two hands which Moore produced in the same way as it covers everything else. The whole question is: Do objects like Moore's two hands qualify as inhabitants of an external world? This is not to say that Moore's argument is completely beside the point; what is wrong is to regard it as an experimental 'proof', for it is not like anything one finds in an experimental discipline. Moore was not making an experiment; he was *reminding* his audience of something, reminding them of the way in which the expression 'external object' is in fact used. And his reminder indicated that the issue in philosophy is not to prove or disprove the existence of a world of external objects but rather to *elucidate the concept* of externality. That there is a connection between this issue and the central philosophical problem about the general nature of reality is, I think, obvious.

### 4.   *The Philosopher's Concern with Language*

So much, at present, for the relation between philosophy and science. But I have yet to show why the rejection of the master-scientist conception of the philosopher need not, and should not, lead to the underlabourer conception. I have spoken of Moore reminding us how certain expressions are in fact used; and I have emphasized how important in philosophy is the notion of elucidating a concept. These are ways of speaking which *prima facie* fit the underlabourer conception very well. And in fact what is wrong with that conception in general is to be looked for not so much in any downright false doctrine as in a systematically mistaken emphasis.

Philosophical issues do, to a large extent, turn on the correct use of certain linguistic expressions; the elucidation of a concept is, to a large extent, the clearing up of linguistic confusions. Nevertheless, the philosopher's concern is not with correct usage as such and not all linguistic confusions are equally relevant to philosophy. They are relevant only in so far as the discussion of them is designed to throw light on the question how far reality is intelligible[1] and what difference would the fact that he could have a grasp of reality make to the life of man. So we have to ask how questions of language, and what kinds of question about language, are likely to bear upon these issues.

To ask whether reality is intelligible is to ask about the relation between thought and reality. In considering the nature of thought one is led also to consider the nature of language. Inseparably bound up with

[1] I am aware that this is a somewhat old-fashioned sounding way to talk. I do so in order to mark the difference between the philosopher's concern with reality and that of, e.g., the scientist. I take this opportunity of saying that I owe the statement of the philosopher's kind of interest in language, in the next paragraph, to an unpublished talk by Mr. Rush Rhees on "Philosophy and Art".

the question whether reality is intelligible, therefore, is the question of how language is connected with reality, of what it is to *say* something. In fact the philosopher's interest in language lies not so much in the solution of particular linguistic confusions for their own sakes, as in the solution of confusions about the nature of language in general.

I will elaborate this point polemically, referring to T. D. Weldon's *Vocabulary of Politics*. I choose this book because in it Weldon uses his interpretation of the concern which philosophy has with language to support a conception of the relations between philosophy and the study of society, which is fundamentally at variance with the conception to be commended in this monograph. Weldon's view is based on an interpretation of recent developments in philosophy in this country. What has occurred, he says, is that 'philosophers have become extremely self-conscious about language. They have come to realise that many of the problems which their predecessors have found insuperable arose not from anything mysterious or inexplicable in the world but from the eccentricities of the language in which we try to describe the world' (35: Chapter I). The problems of social and political philosophy, therefore, arise from the eccentricities of the language in which we try to describe social and political institutions, rather than from anything mysterious in those institutions themselves. In accordance with the under-labourer conception of philosophy, which Weldon is here faithfully following, he regards philosophy as having a purely negative role to play in advancing our understanding of social life. Any positive advances in this understanding must be contributed by the methods of empirical science rather than by those of philosophy. There is no hint that discussion of the central questions of metaphysics and epistemology themselves may (as I shall later argue) have light to throw on the nature of human societies.

In fact those questions are cavalierly brushed aside in the very statement of Weldon's position. To assume at the outset that one can make a sharp distinction between 'the world' and 'the language in which we try to describe the world', to the extent of saying that the problems of philosophy do not arise at all out of the former but only out of the latter, is to beg the whole question of philosophy.

Weldon would no doubt reply that this question has already been settled in a sense favourable to his position by those philosophers who contributed to the developments of which he is speaking. But even if we overlook the important fact that philosophical issues can never be settled in that way, that the results of other men's philosophizing cannot be assumed in one's own philosophical work as can scientific theories established by other men—even, I say, if we overlook this, the work of Wittgenstein, the most outstanding contributor to the philosophical development in question, is just misinterpreted if it is taken to support Weldon's way of speaking. This is obvious enough in relation to Wittgenstein's *Tractatus Logico-Philosophicus*, as can be seen from two representative quotations. 'To give the essence of proposition means to give the essence of all description, therefore the essence of the world' (36: 5.4711). 'That the world is *my* world shows itself in the fact that the limits of my language (of the only language I can understand) mean the limits of *my* world' (*Ibid.*: 5.62).

It is true that these ideas in the *Tractatus* are connected with a theory of language which Wittgenstein afterwards rejected and which Weldon would also reject. But Wittgenstein's methods of argument in the later *Philosophical Investigations* are equally incompatible with any easy distinction between the world and language. This comes out clearly in his treatment of the concept of seeing an object *as* something: for example, seeing the picture of an arrow as in flight. The following passage is characteristic of Wittgenstein's whole approach:

> In the triangle I can see now *this* as apex, *that* as base— now *this* as apex, *that* as base.—Clearly the words 'Now I am seeing this as the apex' cannot so far mean anything to a learner who has only just met the concepts of apex, base, and so on.—But I do not mean this as an empirical proposition.
>
> 'Now he's seeing it like *this*', 'now like *that*' would only be said of someone *capable* of making certain applications of the figure quite freely.
>
> The substratum of this experience is the mastery of a technique.
>
> But how queer for this to be the logical condition of someone's having such and such an *experience*! After all, you don't say that one only 'has toothache' if one is capable of doing such-and-such.—From this it follows that we cannot be dealing with the same concept of experience here. It is a different though related concept.
>
> It is only if someone *can do*, has learnt, is master of, such-and-such, that it makes sense to say he has had *this* experience.
>
> And if this sounds crazy, you need to reflect that the

*concept* of seeing is modified here. (A similar consideration is often necessary to get rid of a feeling of dizziness in mathematics.)

We talk, we utter words, and only *later* get a picture of their life. (37: II, xi.)

We cannot say then, with Weldon, that the problems of philosophy arise out of language *rather than* out of the world, because in discussing language philosophically we are in fact discussing *what counts as belonging to the world*. Our idea of what belongs to the realm of reality is given for us in the language that we use. The concepts we have settle for us the form of the experience we have of the world. It may be worth reminding ourselves of the truism that when we speak of the world we are speaking of what we in fact mean by the expression 'the world': there is no way of getting outside the concepts in terms of which we think of the world, which is what Weldon is trying to do in his statements about the nature of philosophical problems. The world *is* for us what is presented through those concepts. That is not to say that our concepts may not change; but when they do, that means that our concept of the world has changed too.

## 5. *Conceptual and Empirical Enquiries*

This misunderstanding of the way in which philosophical treatments of linguistic confusions are also elucidations of the nature of reality leads to inadequacies in the actual methods used for treating such questions. Empiricists like Weldon systematically underemphasize the extent of what may be said *a priori:* for them all statements about reality must be empirical or they are unfounded, and *a priori* statements are 'about linguistic usage' as opposed to being 'about reality'. But if the integrity of science is endangered by the *over*-estimation of the *a priori*, against which Hume legitimately fought, it is no less true that philosophy is crippled by its *under*estimation: by mistaking conceptual enquiries into what it makes sense to say for empirical enquiries which must wait upon experience for their solution.

The misunderstanding is well illustrated in the following passage from Hume himself. He is discussing the extent and nature of our knowledge of what will happen in the future and arguing that nothing in the future can be logically guaranteed for us by our knowledge of what has been observed to happen in the past.

> In vain do you pretend to have learned the nature of bodies from past experience. Their secret nature, and consequently all their effects and influence may change, without any change in their sensible qualities. This happens sometimes, and with regard to some objects: Why may it not happen always and with regard to all objects? What logic, what process of argument secures you against this supposition? (12: Section IV, Part II.)

Hume assumes here that since a statement about the uniform behaviour of *some* objects is a straightforward empirical matter which may at any time be upset by future experience, the same must be true of a statement about the uniform behaviour of all objects. This assumption is very compelling. Its compellingness derives from a healthy unwillingness to admit that anyone can legislate *a priori* concerning the course of future experience on the basis of purely logical considerations. And of course we cannot thus legislate against a breakdown in the regular order of nature, such as would make scientific work impossible and destroy speech, thought, and even life. But we can and must legislate *a priori* against the possibility of *describing* such a situation in the terms which Hume attempts to use: in terms, that is, of the properties of objects, their causes and effects. For were the order of nature to break down in that way these terms would be no longer applicable. Because there may be minor, or even major, variations *within* such an order without our whole conceptual apparatus being upset, it does not follow that we can use our existing apparatus (and what other are we to use?) to describe a breakdown in the order of nature as a whole.

This is not merely verbal quibbling. For the whole philosophical purport of enquiries like Hume's, is to clarify those concepts which are fundamental to our conception of reality, like *object, property of an object, cause and effect*. To point out that the use of such notions necessarily presupposes the continuing truth of *most* of our generalizations about the behaviour of the world we live in is of central importance to such an undertaking.

The importance of this issue for the philosophy of the social sciences will become more apparent later on. I shall argue, for instance, that many of the more important theoretical issues which have been raised in those studies belong to philosophy rather than to science and are, therefore, to be settled by *a priori* conceptual analysis rather than by empirical research.

For example, the question of what constitutes social behaviour is a demand for an elucidation of the *concept* of social behaviour. In dealing with questions of this sort there should be no question of 'waiting to see' what empirical research will show us; it is a matter of tracing the implications of the concepts we use.

## 6. *The Pivotal Role of Epistemology within Philosophy*

I can now offer an alternative view of the way in which the problems of epistemology and metaphysics are related to those in what I have called the peripheral philosophical disciplines. Everything I have so far said has been based on the assumption that what is really fundamental to philosophy is the question regarding the nature and intelligibility of reality. It is easy to see that this question must lead on to a consideration of what we mean by 'intelligibility' in the first place. What is it to understand something, to grasp the sense of something? Now if we look at the contexts in which the notions of understanding, of making something intelligible, are used we find that these differ widely amongst themselves. Moreover, if those contexts are examined and compared, it soon becomes apparent that the notion of intelligibility is systematically ambiguous (in Professor Ryle's sense of the phrase) in its use in those contexts: that is, its sense varies systematically according to the particular context in which it is being used.

The scientist, for instance, tries to make the world more intelligible; but so do the historian, the religious prophet and the artist; so does the philosopher. And although we may describe the activities of all these kinds of thinker in terms of the concepts of understanding and intelligibility, it is clear that in very many important ways, the objectives of each of them differ from the objectives of any of the others. For instance, I have already tried, in Section 3, to give some account of the differences between the kinds of 'understanding of reality' sought by the philosopher and the scientist respectively.

It does not follow from this that we are just punning when we speak of the activities of all these enquirers in terms of the notion of making things intelligible. That no more follows than does a similar conclusion with regard to the word 'game' when Wittgenstein shows us that there is no set of properties common and peculiar to all the activities correctly so called (Cf. 37: I, 66–71). There is just as much point in saying that science, art, religion and philosophy are all concerned with making things intelligible as there is in saying that football, chess, patience and skipping are all games. But just as it would be foolish to say that all these activities are part of one supergame, if only we were clever enough to learn how to play it, so is it foolish to suppose that the results of all those other activities should all add up to one grand theory of reality (as some philosophers have imagined: with the corollary that it was their job to discover it).

On my view then, the philosophy of science will be concerned with the kind of understanding sought and conveyed by the scientist; the philosophy of religion will be concerned with the way in which religion attempts to present an intelligible picture of the world; and so on. And of course these activities and their aims will be mutually compared and contrasted. The purpose of such philosophical enquiries will be to contribute to our understanding of what is involved in the concept of intelligibility, so that we may better understand what it means to call reality intelligible. It is important for my purposes to note how different is this from the underlabourer conception. In particular, the philosophy of science (or of whatever enquiry may be in question) is presented here as autonomous, and not parasitic on science itself, as far as the provenance of its problems is concerned. The motive force for the philosophy of science comes from within philosophy rather than from within science. And its aim is not merely the negative one of removing obstacles from the path to the acquisition of further scientific knowledge, but the positive one of an increased philosophical understanding of what is involved in the concept of intelligibility. The difference between these conceptions is more than a verbal one.

It might appear at first sight as if no room had been left for metaphysics and epistemology. For if the concept of intelligibility (and, I should add, the concept of reality equally) are systematically ambiguous as between different intellectual disciplines, does not the philosophical task of giving an account of those notions disintegrate into the philosophies of the various disciplines in question? Does not the idea of a *special* study of epistemology rest on the false idea that all varieties of the notion of intelligibility can be reduced to a single set of criteria?

That is a false conclusion to draw, though it does provide a salutary warning against expecting from epistemology the formulation of a set of *criteria* of intelligibility. Its task will rather be to describe the conditions which must be satisfied if there are to *be* any criteria of understanding at all.


## 7.  *Epistemology and the Understanding of Society*

I should like here to give a preliminary indication of how this epistemological undertaking may be expected to bear upon our understanding of social life. Let us consider again Burnet's formulation of the main question of philosophy. He asks what difference it will make to the life of man if his mind can have contact with reality. Let us first interpret this question in the most superficially obvious way: it is clear that men do decide how they shall behave on the basis of their view of what is the case in the world around them. For instance, a man who has to catch an early morning train will set his alarm clock in accordance with his belief about the time at which the train is due to leave. If anyone is inclined to object to this example on the grounds of its triviality, let him reflect on the difference that is made to human life by the fact that there are such things as alarm clocks and trains running to schedule, and methods of determining the truth of statements about the times of trains, and so on. The concern of philosophy here is with the question: What is involved in 'having knowledge' of facts like these, and what is the general nature of behaviour which is decided on in accordance with such knowledge?

The nature of this question will perhaps be clearer if it is compared with another question concerning the importance in human life of knowing the world as it really is. I am thinking of the moral question which so exercised Ibsen in such plays as *The Wild Duck* and *Ghosts*: How far is it important to a man's life that he should live it in clear awareness of the facts of his situation and of his relations to those around him? In *Ghosts* this question is presented by considering a man whose life is being ruined by his ignorance of the truth about his heredity. *The Wild Duck* starts from the opposite direction: here is a man who is living a perfectly contented life which is, however, based on a complete misunderstanding of the attitude to him of those he knows; should he be disillusioned and have his happiness disrupted in the interests of truth? It is necessary to notice that our understanding of both these issues depends on our recognition of the *prima facie* importance of understanding the situation in which one lives one's life. The question in *The Wild Duck* is not whether that is important, but whether or not it is *more* important than being happy.

Now the interest of the epistemologist in such situations will be to throw light on *why* such an understanding should have this importance in a man's life by showing what is involved in having it. To use a Kantian phrase, his interest will be in the question: How is such an understanding (or indeed any understanding) possible? To answer this question it is necessary to show the central role which the concept of understanding plays in the activities which are characteristic of human societies. In this way the discussion of what an understanding of reality consists in merges into the discussion of the difference the possession of such an understanding may be expected to make to the life of man; and this again involves a consideration of the general nature of a human society, an analysis, that is, of the concept of a human society.

A man's social relations with his fellows are permeated with his ideas about reality. Indeed, 'permeated' is hardly a strong enough word: social relations are expressions of ideas about reality. In the Ibsen situations which I just referred to, for example, it would be impossible to delineate the character's attitudes to the people surrounding him except in terms of his ideas about what they think of him, what they have done in the past, what they are likely to do in the future, and so on; and, in *Ghosts*, his ideas about how he is biologically related to them. Again, a monk has certain characteristic social relations with his fellow monks and with people outside the monastery; but it would be impossible to give more than a superficial account of those relations without taking into account the religious ideas around which the monk's life revolves.

At this point it becomes clearer how the line of approach which I am commending conflicts with widely held conceptions of sociology and of the social studies generally. It conflicts, for instance, with the view of Emile Durkheim:

> I consider extremely fruitful this idea that social life should be explained, not by the notions of those who participate in it, but by more profound causes which are unperceived by consciousness, and I think also that these causes are to be sought mainly in the manner according to which the associated individuals are grouped. Only in this way, it seems, can history become a science, and sociology

itself exist. [See Durkheim's review of A. Labriola: 'Essais sur la conception materialiste de l'histoire' in *Revue Philosophique*, December, 1897.]

It conflicts too with von Wiese's conception of the task of sociology as being to give an account of social life 'disregarding the cultural aims of individuals in society in order to study the influences which they exert on each other as a result of community life'. (See 2: p. 8.)

The crucial question here, of course, is how far any sense can be given to Durkheim's idea of 'the manner according to which associated individuals are grouped' *apart* from the 'notions' of such individuals; or how far it makes sense to speak of individuals exerting influence on each other (in von Wiese's conception) in abstraction from such individuals' 'cultural aims'. I shall try to deal explicitly with these central questions at a later stage in the argument. At present I simply wish to point out that positions like these do in fact come into conflict with philosophy, conceived as an enquiry into the nature of man's knowledge of reality and into the difference which the possibility of such knowledge makes to human life.

## 8. *Rules: Wittgenstein's Analysis*

I must now attempt a more detailed picture of the way in which the epistemological discussion of man's understanding of reality throws light on the nature of human society and of social relations between men. To that end I propose to give some account of the light which has been shed on the epistemological issue by

Wittgenstein's discussion of the concept of *following a rule* in the *Philosophical Investigations*.

Burnet spoke of the mind's 'contact' with reality. Let us take an obvious *prima facie* case of such contact and consider what is involved in it. Suppose that I am wondering in what year Everest was first climbed; I think to myself: 'Mount Everest was climbed in 1953'. What I want to ask here is what is meant by saying that I am 'thinking about Mount Everest?' How is my thought related to the thing, namely Mount Everest, about which I am thinking? Let us make the issue somewhat sharper yet. In order to remove complications about the function of mental images in such situations I will suppose that I express my thought explicitly in words. The appropriate question then becomes: what is it about my utterance of the words 'Mount Everest' which makes it possible to say I *mean* by those words a certain peak in the Himalayas. I have introduced the subject in this somewhat round-about way in order to bring out the connection between the question about the nature of the 'contact' which the mind has with reality and the question about the nature of meaning. I have chosen as an example of a word being used to mean something a case where the word in question is being used to *refer* to something, not because I assign any special logical or metaphysical priority to this type of meaning, but solely because in this case the connection between the question about the nature of meaning and that about the relation between thought and reality is particularly striking.

A natural first answer to give is that I am able to mean what I do by the words 'Mount Everest' because they have been defined to me. There are all sorts of

ways in which this may have been done: I may have
been shown Mount Everest on a map, I may have been
told that it is the highest peak in the world; or I may
have been flown over the Himalayas in an aeroplane
and had the actual Everest pointed out to me. To
eliminate further complications let us make the last
supposition; that is, to use the technical terminology of
logic, let us concentrate on the case of *ostensive*
definition.

The position then is this. I have had Everest
pointed out to me; I have been told that its name is
'Everest'; and in virtue of those actions in the past I
am now able to *mean* by the words 'Mount Everest'
that peak in the Himalayas. So far so good. But now
we have to ask a further question: What is the connection between those acts in the past and my utterance
of the words 'Mount Everest' now which now gives
this utterance of mine the meaning it has? How, in
general, is a definition connected with the subsequent
use of the expression defined? What is it to 'follow' a
definition? Again there is a superficially obvious
answer to this: the definition lays down the meaning
and to use a word in its correct meaning is to use it in
the same way as that laid down in the definition. And
in a sense, of course, that answer is perfectly correct
and unexceptionable; its only defect is that it does not
remove the philosophical puzzlement. For what is it
to use the word *in the same way* as that laid down in
the definition? How do I decide whether a given pro-
posed use is the same as or different from that laid
down in the definition?

That is not a merely idle question, as can be seen
from the following consideration. As far as immediate

external appearances go, the ostensive definition simply consisted in a gesture and a sound uttered as we were flying over the Himalayas. But suppose that, with that gesture, my teacher had been defining the word 'mountain' for me, rather than 'Everest', as might have been the case, say, had I been in the process of learning English? In that case too my grasp of the correct meaning of the word 'mountain' would be manifested in my continuing to use it in the same way as that laid down in the definition. Yet the correct use of the word 'mountain' is certainly not the same as the correct use of the word 'Everest'! So apparently the word 'same' presents us with another example of systematic ambiguity: we do not know whether two things are to be regarded as the same or not unless we are told the context in which the question arises. However much we may be tempted to think otherwise, there is no absolute unchanging sense to the words 'the same'.

> But isn't *the same* at least the same?
> We seem to have an infallible paradigm of identity in the identity of a thing with itself. I feel like saying: 'Here at any rate there can't be any variety of interpretations. If you are seeing a thing you are seeing identity too'.
> Then are two things the same when they are what one thing is? And how am I to apply what the *one* thing shows me to the case of two things? (37: I, 215.)

I said that the particular interpretation which is to be put upon the words 'the same' depends on the context in which the question arises. That may be expressed more precisely. It is only in terms of a given *rule* that we can attach a specific sense to the words 'the same'. In terms of the rule governing the use of

the word 'mountain', a man who uses it to refer to
Mount Everest on one occasion and to Mont Blanc on
another occasion is using it in the same way each
time; but someone who refers to Mont Blanc as
'Everest' would not be said to be using this word in
the same way as someone who used it to refer to
Mount Everest. So the question: What is it for a word
to have a meaning? leads on to the question: What is
it for someone to follow a rule?

Let us once again start by considering the obvious
answer. We should like to say: someone is following a
rule if he always acts in the same way on the same kind
of occasion. But this again, though correct, does not
advance matters since, as we have seen, it is only in
terms of a given rule that the word 'same' acquires a
definite sense. 'The use of the word "rule" and the use
of the word "same" are interwoven. (As are the use of
"proposition" and the use of "true".)' (37: I, 225.)   So
the problem becomes : How is the word 'same' to
be given a sense?; or: In what circumstances does it
make sense to say of somebody that he is following a
rule in what he does?

Suppose that the word 'Everest' has just been
ostensively defined to me. It might be thought that I
could settle at the outset what is to count as the
correct use of this word in the future by making a
conscious decision to the effect: 'I will use this word
only to refer to *this* mountain'. And that of course, in
the context of the language which we all speak and
understand, is perfectly intelligible. But, just because
it presupposes the settled institution of the language
we all speak and understand, this does not throw any
light on the philosophical difficulty. Obviously we are

not permitted to presuppose that whose very possibility we are investigating. It is just as difficult to give any account of what is meant by 'acting in accordance with my decision' as it is to give an account of what it was to 'act in accordance with the ostensive definition' in the first place. However emphatically I point at this mountain here before me and however emphatically I utter the words 'this mountain', my decision still has to be *applied* in the future, and it is precisely what is involved in such an application that is here in question. Hence no *formula* will help to solve this problem; we must always come to a point at which we have to give an account of the application of the formula.

What is the difference between someone who is really applying a rule in what he does and someone who is not? A difficulty here is that any series of actions which a man may perform can be brought within the scope of some formula or other if we are prepared to make it sufficiently complicated. Yet, that a man's actions *might* be interpreted as an application of a given formula, is in itself no guarantee that he is in fact applying that formula. What is the difference between those cases?

Imagine a man—let us call him *A*—writing down the following figures on a blackboard: 1 3 5 7. *A* now asks his friend, *B*, how the series is to be continued. Almost everybody in this situation, short of having special reasons to be suspicious, would answer: 9 11 13 15. Let us suppose that *A* refuses to accept this as a continuation of his series, saying it runs as follows: 1 3 5 7 1 3 5 7 9 11 13 15 9 11 13 15. He then asks *B* to continue from there. At this point *B* has a variety of alternatives to choose from. Let us suppose that he makes a choice and that *A* again refuses to accept it, but substitutes another continuation of his own. And let us suppose that this continues for some time. There would undoubtedly come a point at which *B*, with perfect justification, would say that *A* was not really following a *mathematical* rule at all, even though all the continuations he had made to date *could* be brought within the scope of some formula. Certainly *A* was following a rule; but his rule was: Always to substitute a continuation different from the one suggested by *B* at every stage. And though this is a perfectly good rule of its kind, it does not belong to arithmetic.

Now *B*'s eventual reaction, and the fact that it would be quite justified, particularly if several other individuals were brought into the game and if *A* always refused to allow their suggested continuations as correct—all this suggests a very important feature of the concept of following a rule. It suggests that one has to take account not only of the actions of the person whose behaviour is in question as a candidate for the category of rule-following, but also the *reactions of other people* to what he does. More specifically, it is only in a situation in which it makes sense to suppose that somebody else could in principle discover the rule which I am following that I can intelligibly be said to follow a rule at all.

Let us consider this more closely. It is important to remember that when *A* wrote down: 1 3 5 7, *B* (representing anyone who has learnt elementary arithmetic) continued the series by writing: 9 11 13 15, etc., *as a matter of course*. The very fact that I have been able to write 'etc.' after those figures and that I can be confident of being taken in one way rather than another by virtually all my readers, is itself a demonstration of the same point. 'The rule can only seem to me to produce all its consequences in advance if I draw them *as a matter of course.* As much as it is a matter of course for me to call this colour "blue".' (37: I, 238.) It should be understood that these remarks are not confined to the case of mathematical formulae but apply to all cases of rule-following. They apply, for instance, to the use of words like 'Everest' and 'mountain': given a certain sort of training everybody does, as a matter of course, continue to use these words in the same way as would everybody else.

It is this that makes it possible for us to attach a sense to the expression 'the same' in a given context. It is extremely important to notice here that going on in one way rather than another as a matter of course must not be just a peculiarity of the person whose behaviour claims to be a case of rule-following. His behaviour belongs to that category only if it is possible for someone else to grasp what he is doing, by being brought to the pitch of himself going on in that way as a matter of course.

Imagine someone using a line as a rule in the following way: he holds a pair of compasses, and carries one of its points along the line that is the 'rule', while the other one draws the line that follows the rule. And while he moves along the ruling line he alters the opening of the compasses, apparently with great precision, looking at the rule the whole time as if it determined what he did. And watching him we see no kind of regularity in this opening and shutting of the compasses. We cannot learn his way of following the line from it. Here perhaps one really would say: 'The original seems to *intimate* to him which way he is to go. But it is not a rule'. (37: I, 237.)

Why is it not a rule? Because the notion of following a rule is logically inseparable from the notion of *making a mistake*. If it is possible to say of someone that he is following a rule that means that one can ask whether he is doing what he does correctly or not. Otherwise there is no foothold in his behaviour in which the notion of a rule can take a grip; there is then no *sense* in describing his behaviour in that way, since everything he does is as good as anything else he might do, whereas the point of the concept of a rule is that it should enable us to *evaluate* what is being done.

Let us consider what is involved in making a mistake (which includes, of course, a consideration of what is involved in doing something correctly). A mistake is a contravention of what is *established* as correct; as such, it must be *recognisable* as such a contravention. That is, if I make a mistake in, say, my use of a word, other people must be able to point it out to me. If this is not so, I can do what I like and there is no external check on what I do; that is, nothing is established. Establishing a standard is not an activity which it makes sense to ascribe to any individual in complete isolation from other individuals. For it is contact with other individuals which alone makes possible the external check on one's actions which is inseparable from an established standard.

A qualification must be made here to avert a possible misunderstanding. It is, of course, possible, within a human society as we know it, with its established language and institutions, for an individual to adhere to a *private* rule of conduct. What Wittgenstein insists on, however, is, first, that it must be in principle possible for other people to grasp that rule and judge when it is being correctly followed; secondly, that it makes no sense to suppose anyone capable of establishing a purely personal standard of behaviour *if* he had never had any experience of human society with its socially established rules. In this part of philosophy one is concerned with the *general concept* of following a rule; that being so, one is not at liberty, in explaining what is involved in that concept, to take for granted a situation in which that concept is already presupposed.

## 9. *Some Misunderstandings of Wittgenstein*

The necessity for rules to have a social setting is particularly important in connection with the philosophical problem about the nature of sensations. For it implies that the language in which we speak about our sensations must be governed by criteria which are publicly accessible; those criteria cannot rest in something essentially private to a given individual, as many philosophers have supposed. Wittgenstein's discussion in the *Philosophical Investigations* is intimately bound up with this special problem. But, as P. F. Strawson points out, Wittgenstein's arguments apply equally against the idea of *any* language which is not, at some point, based on a common life in which many individuals participate. Strawson regards this fact as an objection to Wittgenstein's position for, he alleges, it rules out as inconceivable something we can in fact perfectly well conceive. He argues that we can quite well imagine, as a logical possibility, a desert-islander who has never been brought up in a human society devising a language for his own use. We can also, he says, imagine the introduction of an observer (B) of the user of this language who

> observes a correlation between the use of its words and sentences and the speaker's actions and environment. . . . Observer B is thus able to form hypotheses about the meanings (the regular use) of the words of his subject's language. He might in time come to be able to speak it: then the practice of each serves as a check on the practice of the other. But shall we say that, before this fortunate result was achieved (before the use of the language becomes a *shared* 'form of life'), the words of the language had no meaning, no use? (32: p. 85.)

To Strawson it seems self-evidently absurd to say such a thing. The persuasiveness of his position lies in the fact that he appears to have succeeded in giving a coherent description of a situation which, on Wittgenstein's principles, ought to be indescribable because inconceivable. But this is only appearance; in fact Strawson has begged the whole question. His description is vitiated at the outset as a contribution to the problem under discussion by containing terms the applicability of which is precisely what is in question: terms like 'language', 'use', 'words', 'sentences', 'meaning'—and all without benefit of quotation marks. To say that observer B may 'form hypotheses about the meanings (the regular use) of the words in his subject's language' is senseless unless one can speak of what his subject is doing in terms of the concepts of meaning, language, use, etc. From the fact that we can observe him going through certain motions and making certain sounds—which, were they to be performed by somebody else in another context, that of a human society, it would be quite legitimate to describe in those terms, it by no means follows that *his* activities are legitimately so describable. And the fact that B might correlate his subject's practices with his own does not establish Strawson's point; for the whole substance of Wittgenstein's argument is that it is not those practices considered on their own which justify the application of categories like language and meaning, but the social *context* in which those practices are performed. Strawson says nothing to controvert those arguments.

This is well brought out by Norman Malcolm. As he says, Strawson's 'language-user' might utter a sound each time a cow appeared; but what we need to ask is what makes that sound a *word* and what makes it the word for a *cow*. A parrot might go through just the same motions and we should still not say he was talking (with understanding). 'It is as if Strawson thought: There is no difficulty about it; the man just *makes* the mark refer to a sensation' (or, in this instance, just *makes* the sound refer to a cow). (16: p. 554). But this at once raises all the difficulties discussed in the last section; it is precisely the nature of the connection between an initial definition and the subsequent use of a sound that is in question.

A. J. Ayer makes very similar objections to Wittgenstein's position. Like Strawson he is prone to describe the activities of his hypothetical 'unsocialized' Crusoe in terms which derive their sense from a social context. Consider, for instance, the following passage:

> He (that is, 'Crusoe') may think that a bird which he sees flying past is a bird of the same type as one which he has previously named, when in fact it is of a very different type, sufficiently different for him to have given it a different name if he had observed it more closely. (4).

This of course presupposes that it makes sense to speak of 'naming' in such a context; and all the difficulties about the sense we are to attach to the notion of *sameness* are raised in a particularly acute form by the phrase 'sufficiently different for him to have given it a different name'. For a 'sufficient difference' is certainly not something that is given for one absolutely in the object one is observing; it gets its sense only from the particular rule one happens to be following. But it is essential for Ayer's argument that this should have a sense independent of any particular rule, for he is trying to use it as a foundation on which to build the possibility of a rule independent of any social context.

Ayer also argues that 'some human being must have been the first to use a symbol'. He wishes to imply by this that socially established rules clearly cannot have been presupposed by *this* use; and if that were so, of course, established rules cannot be a logically necessary prerequisite of the use of symbols in general. The argument is attractive, but fallacious. From the fact that there must have been a transition from a state of affairs where there was no language to a state of affairs in which there was language, it by no means follows that there must have been some individual who was the first to use language. This is just as absurd as the argument that there must have been some individual who was the first to take part in a tug-of-war; more so, in fact. The supposition that language was *invented* by any individual is quite nonsensical, as is well shown by Rush Rhees in his reply to Ayer. (28: p. 85–87.) We can imagine practices gradually growing up amongst early men none of which could count as the invention of language; and yet once these practices had reached a certain degree of sophistication— it would be a misunderstanding to ask *what* degree precisely —one can say of such people that they have a language. This whole issue involves an application of something like the Hegelian principle of a change in quantity leading to a difference in quality, which I will discuss more fully at a later stage.

There is one counter-argument to Wittgenstein's position to which Ayer seems to attach peculiar importance, since he uses it not only in the paper to which I have been referring but also in his later book, *The Problem of Knowledge*. One of Wittgenstein's most important arguments runs as follows:

> Let us imagine a table (something like a dictionary) that exists only in our imagination. A dictionary can be used to justify the translation of a word X into a word Y. But are we also to call it a justification if such a table is to be looked up only in the imagination?—'Well, yes; then it is a subjective justification.'—But justification consists in appealing to something independent.—'But surely I can appeal from one memory to another. For example, I don't know if I have remembered the time of departure of a train

right and to check it I call to mind how a page of the time-table looked. Isn't it the same here?'—No; for this process has got to produce a memory which is actually *correct*. If the mental image of the time-table could not itself be *tested* for correctness, how could it confirm the correctness of the first memory? (As if someone were to buy several copies of the morning paper to assure himself that what it said was true.)

Looking up a table in the imagination is no more looking up a table than the image of the result of an imagined experiment is the result of an experiment. (37: I, 265.)

Ayer's counter-argument is that *any* use of language, no matter how publicly established, is open to the same difficulty; for, he says, even if one's use of a word on a particular occasion is ratified by other language-users, one still has to *identify* what they say. 'No doubt mistakes can always occur; but if one never accepted any identification without a further check, one would never identify anything at all. And then no descriptive use of language would be possible.' (3: Chapter 2, Section V.) Strawson also seems to think that Wittgenstein is open to such an objection for he asks, pointedly, in connection with Wittgenstein's arguments: 'Do we ever in fact find ourselves mis-remembering the use of very *simple* words of our common language, and having to correct ourselves by attention to others' use?' (32: p. 85.)

But this objection is misconceived; Wittgenstein does not say that every act of identification in fact needs a further check in the sense that we can never rest contented with our judgments. That so obviously leads to an infinite regress that it is difficult to imagine anyone maintaining it who did not want to establish a system of complete Pyrrhonean scepticism such as is very far indeed from Wittgenstein's intention. In fact Wittgenstein himself is very insistent that 'Justifications have to come to an end somewhere'; and this is a foundation stone of many of his most characteristic doctrines: as for instance his treatment of the 'matter of course' way in which rules are, in general, followed. Ayer and Strawson have misunderstood Wittgenstein's insistence that it must be *possible* for the judgment of a single individual to be checked by independent criteria (criteria that are established independently of that individual's will); it is only in special circumstances that such a check *actually* has to be made. But the fact that it can be done if necessary makes a difference to what can be said about those cases in which it needs not to be done. A single use of language does not stand alone; it is intelligible only within the general context in which language is used; and an important part of that context is the procedure of correcting mistakes when they occur and checking when a mistake is suspected.

———◆———

# CHAPTER TWO

# THE NATURE OF MEANINGFUL
# BEHAVIOUR

## 1. *Philosophy and Sociology*

IN Section 7 of the last chapter I tried to indicate in a general way how philosophy, conceived as the study of the nature of man's understanding of reality, may be expected to illuminate the nature of human interrelations in society. The discussion of Wittgenstein in Sections 8 and 9 has borne out that presumption. For it has shown that the philosophical elucidation of human intelligence, and the notions associated with this, requires that these notions be placed in the context of the relations between men in society. In so far as there has been a genuine revolution in philosophy in recent years, perhaps it lies in the emphasis on that fact and in the profound working out of its consequences, which we find in Wittgenstein's work. 'What has to be accepted, the given, is—so one could say—forms of life.' (37: II, xi, p. 226e.)

I said earlier that the relation between epistemology and the peripheral branches of philosophy was that the former concerned the general conditions under which it is possible to speak of understanding while the latter concerned the peculiar forms which understanding takes in particular kinds of context. Wittgenstein's remark suggests a possibility of rephrasing this: whereas the philosophies of science, of art, of history, etc., will have the task of elucidating the peculiar natures of those forms of life called 'science', 'art', etc., epistemology will try to elucidate what is involved in the notion of a form of life as such. Wittgenstein's analysis of the concept of following a rule and his account of the peculiar kind of interpersonal agreement which this involves is a contribution to that epistemological elucidation.

This conclusion has important consequences for our conception of the social studies; particularly the theoretical part of general sociology and the foundations of social psychology. As is well known, there has always been some dispute about the role which sociology ought to play *vis-à-vis* the other social studies. Some have thought that sociology should be the social science *par excellence*, synthesising the results of special social studies, like economic and political theory, into a unified theory of society in general. Others, however, have wanted to regard sociology simply as one social science on the same level as all the others, confined to a restricted subject-matter of its own. However, whichever of these views one adopts, one can in the end hardly avoid including in sociology a discussion of the nature of social phenomena in general; and this is bound to occupy a special place amongst the various disciplines devoted to the study of society. For all these disciplines are in one way or another concerned with social phenomena and require, therefore, a clear grasp of what is involved in the concept of a social phenomenon. Moreover,

> all the subjects of investigation which are attributed to sociology, urbanism, race contacts, social stratification, or the relations between social conditions and mental constructions (*Wissenssoziologie*), are in fact difficult to isolate, and have the character of *total* phenomena which are connected with society as a whole and with the nature of society. (2: p. 119.)

But to understand the nature of social phenomena in general, to elucidate, that is, the concept of a 'form of life', has been shown to be precisely the aim of epistemology. It is true that the epistemologist's starting point is rather different from that of the sociologist but, if Wittgenstein's arguments are sound, that is what he must sooner or later concern himself with. That means that the relations between sociology and epistemology must be different from, and very much closer than, what is usually imagined to be the case. The accepted view runs, I think, roughly as follows. Any intellectual discipline may, at one time or another, run into philosophical difficulties, which often herald a revolution in the fundamental theories and which form temporary obstacles in the path of advancing scientific enquiry. The difficulties in the conception of simultaneity which Einstein had to face and which presaged the formulation of the revolutionary Special Theory of Relativity, provide an example. Those difficulties bore many of the characteristics which one associates with philosophical puzzlement and they were notably different from the technical theoretical problems which are solved in the normal process of advancing scientific enquiry. Now it is often supposed that newly developing disciplines, with no settled basis of theory on which to build further research, are particularly prone to throw up philosophical puzzles; but that this is a temporary stage which should be lived through and then shaken off as soon as possible. But, in my view, it would be wrong to say this of sociology; for the philosophical problems which arise there are not tiresome foreign bodies which must be removed before sociology can advance on its own independent scientific lines. On the contrary, the central problem of sociology, that of giving an account of the nature of social phenomena in general, itself belongs to philosophy. In fact, not to put too fine a point on it, this part of sociology is really misbegotten epistemology. I say 'misbegotten' because its problems have been largely misconstrued, and therefore mishandled, as a species of scientific problem.

The usual treatment of language in textbooks of social psychology shows the inadequacies to which this may lead. The problem of what language is is clearly of vital importance for sociology in that, with it, one is face to face with the whole question of the characteristic way in which human beings interact with each other in society. Yet the important questions are usually left untouched. One finds examples of the ways in which analogous concepts may differ in the languages of different societies with, perhaps, some indication of the ways in which these differences correspond to differences in the main interests which

are characteristic of the life carried on in those societies.
All this can be interesting and even illuminating
if brought forward by way of illustration in
discussing what it is, after all, for people to have a
language at all. But this one hardly ever meets.
Instead, the notion of having a language, and the
notions that go along with that: such as meaning,
intelligibility, and so on—these are taken for granted.
The impression given is that first there is language
(with words having a meaning, statements capable of
being true or false) and then, this being given, it
comes to enter into human relationships and to be
modified by the particular human relationships into
which it does so enter. What is missed is that those
very categories of meaning, etc., are *logically* depend-
ent for their sense on social interaction between men.
Social psychologists sometimes pay lip-service to this.
We are told, for instance, that 'Concepts are products
of interaction of many people carrying on the important business of living together in groups' (30: p. 456).
But the authors go no further with this than to remark
on the way in which *particular* concepts may reflect
the peculiar life of the society in which they are
current. There is no discussion of how the very
existence of concepts depends on group-life. And they
show that they do not understand the force of this
question when they speak of concepts 'embodying
generalizations'; for one cannot explain what concepts
are in terms of the notion of a generalization. People
do not first make generalizations and then embody
them in concepts: it is only by virtue of their possession of concepts that they are able to make generalizations at all.

## 2. *Meaningful Behaviour*

Wittgenstein's account of what it is to follow a rule is, for obvious reasons, given principally with an eye to elucidating the nature of language. I have now to show how this treatment may shed light on other forms of human interaction besides speech. The forms of activity in question are, naturally, those to which analogous categories are applicable: those, that is, of which we can sensibly say that they have a *meaning*, a *symbolic* character. In the words of Max Weber, we are concerned with human behaviour 'if and in so far as the agent or agents associate a subjective *sense* (*Sinn*) with it'. (33: Chapter I.) I want now to consider what is involved in this idea of meaningful behaviour.

Weber says that the 'sense' of which he speaks is something which is 'subjectively intended'; and he says that the notion of meaningful behaviour is closely associated with notions like *motive* and *reason*. ' "Motive" means a meaningful configuration of circumstances which, to the agent or observer, appears as a meaningful "reason" (*Grund*) of the behaviour in question.' (*Ibid.*)

Let us consider some examples of actions which are performed *for a reason*. Suppose that it is said of a certain person, *N*, that he voted Labour at the last General Election because he thought that a Labour government would be the most likely to preserve industrial peace. What kind of explanation is this? The clearest case is that in which *N*, prior to voting, has discussed the pros and cons of voting Labour and has explicitly come to the conclusion: 'I will vote Labour because that is the best way to preserve industrial peace'. That is a paradigm case of someone performing an action for a reason. To say this is not to deny that in some cases, even where $N$ has gone through such an explicit process of reasoning, it may be possible to dispute whether the reason he has given is in fact the real reason for his behaviour. But there is very often no room for doubt; and if this were not so, the idea of *a reason for an action* would be in danger of completely losing its sense. (This point will assume greater importance subsequently, when I come to discuss the work of Pareto.)

The type of case which I have taken as a paradigm is not the only one covered by Weber's concept. But the paradigm exhibits clearly one feature which I believe to have a more general importance. Suppose that an observer, $O$, is offering the above explanation for $N$'s having voted Labour: then it should be noted that the force of $O$'s explanation rests on the fact that the concepts which appear in it must be grasped not merely by $O$ and his hearers, but also *by N himself*. $N$ must have some idea of what it is to 'preserve industrial peace' and of a connection between this and the kind of government which he expects to be in power if Labour is elected. (For my present purposes it is unnecessary to raise the question whether $N$'s beliefs in a particular instance are true or not.)

Not all cases of meaningful behaviour are as clearcut as this. Here are some intermediate examples. $N$ may not, prior to casting his vote, have formulated any reason for voting as he does. But this does not necessarily preclude the possibility of saying that he has a reason for voting Labour and of specifying that reason. And in this case, just as much as in the paradigm, the acceptability of such an explanation is contingent on $N$'s grasp of the concepts contained in it. If $N$ does not grasp the concept of industrial peace it must be senseless to say that his reason for doing anything is a desire to see industrial peace promoted.

A type of case even farther removed from my paradigm is that discussed by Freud in *The Psychopathology of Everyday Life*. $N$ forgets to post a letter and insists, even after reflection, that this was 'just an oversight' and had no reason. A Freudian observer might insist that $N$ 'must have had a reason' even though it was not apparent to $N$: suggesting perhaps that $N$ unconsciously connected the posting of the letter with something in his life which is painful and which he wants to suppress. In Weberian terms, Freud classifies as 'meaningfully directed' (*sinnhaft orientiert*) actions which have no sense at all to the casual observer. Weber seems to refer to cases of this sort when, in his discussion of borderline cases, he speaks of actions the sense of which is apparent only 'to the expert'. This means that his characterization of *Sinn* as something 'subjectively intended' must be approached warily: more warily, for instance than it is approached by Morris Ginsberg, who appears to assume that Weber is saying that the sociologist's understanding of the behaviour of other people must rest on an analogy with his own introspective experience. (See 11: pp. 153 ff.) This misunderstanding of Weber is very common both among his critics and among his vulgarizing followers; I will say more about it at a later stage. But Weber's insistence on the importance of the subjective point of view can be interpreted in a way which is not open to Ginsberg's objections: he can be taken as meaning that even explanations of the Freudian type, if they are to be acceptable, must be in terms of concepts which are familiar to the agent as well as to the observer. It would make no sense to say that $N$'s omission to post a letter to $X$ (in settlement, say, of a debt) was an expression of $N$'s unconscious resentment against $X$ for having been promoted over his head, if $N$ did not himself understand what was meant by 'obtaining promotion over somebody's head'. It is worth mentioning here too that, in seeking explanations of this sort in the course of psychotherapy, Freudians try to get the patient himself to recognize the validity of the proffered explanation; that this indeed is almost a condition of its being accepted as the 'right' explanation.

The category of meaningful behaviour extends also to actions for which the agent has no 'reason' or 'motive' at all in any of the senses so far discussed. In the first chapter of *Wirtschaft und Gesellschaft* Weber contrasts meaningful action with action which is 'purely reactive' (*bloss reaktiv*) and says that purely *traditional* behaviour is on the borderline between these two categories. But, as Talcott Parsons points out, Weber is not consistent in what he says about this. Sometimes he seems to regard traditional behaviour as simply a species of habit, whereas at other times he sees it as 'a type of social action, its traditionalism consisting in the fixity of certain essentials, their immunity from rational or other criticism'. (24: Chapter XVI.) Economic behaviour related to a fixed standard of living is cited as an example: behaviour, that is, where a man does not exploit an increase in the productive capacities of his labour in order to raise his standard of living but does less work instead. Parsons remarks that tradition in this sense is not to be equated with mere habit, but has a *normative* character. That is, the tradition is regarded as a standard which directs choices between alternative actions. As such it clearly falls within the category of the *sinnhaft*.

Suppose that $N$ votes Labour without deliberating and without subsequently being able to offer any reasons, however hard he is pressed. Suppose that he is simply following without question the example of his father and his friends, who have always voted Labour. (This case must be distinguished from that in which $N$'s *reason* for voting Labour is that his father and friends have always done so.) Now although $N$ does not act here for any reason, his act still has a definite sense. What he does is not *simply* to make a mark on a piece of paper; he is *casting a vote*. And what I want to ask is, what gives his action *this* sense, rather than, say, that of being a move in a game or part of a religious ritual. More generally, by what criteria do we distinguish acts which have a sense from those which do not?

In the paper entitled *R. Stammlers 'Ueberwindung' der materialistischen Geschichtsauffassung*, Weber considers the hypothetical case of two 'non-social' beings meeting and, in a purely physical sense, 'exchanging' objects. (See 34.) This occurrence, he says, is conceivable as an act of *economic* exchange only if it has a sense. He expands this by saying that the present

actions of the two men must carry with them, or
represent, a regulation of their future behaviour.
Action with a sense is symbolic: it goes together with
certain other actions in the sense that it *commits* the
agent to behaving in one way rather than another in
the future. This notion of 'being committed' is most
obviously appropriate where we are dealing with
actions which have an immediate social significance,
like economic exchange or promise-keeping.   But it
applies also to meaningful behaviour of a more
'private' nature. Thus, to stay with examples used by
Weber, if $N$ places a slip of paper between the leaves
of a book he can be said to be 'using a bookmark' only
if he acts with the idea of using the slip to determine
where he shall start re-reading. This does not mean
that he must necessarily *actually* so use it in the future
(though that is the paradigm case); the point is that if
he does not, some special explanation will be called
for, such as that he forgot, changed his mind, or got
tired of the book.

The notion of being committed by what I do now to
doing something else in the future is identical in form
with the connection between a definition and the
subsequent use of the word defined, which I discussed
in the last chapter. It follows that I can only be
committed in the future by what I do now if my
present act is the *application of a rule*. Now according
to the argument of the last chapter, this is possible
only where the act in question has a relation to a
social context: this must be true even of the most
private acts, if, that is, they are meaningful.

Let us return to $N$'s exercise of his vote: its
possibility rests on two presuppositions. In the first

place, $N$ must live in a society which has certain specific political institutions—a parliament which is constituted in a certain way and a government which is related in a certain way to the parliament. If he lives in a society whose political structure is patriarchal, it will clearly make no sense to speak of him as 'voting' for a particular government, however much his action may resemble in appearance that of a voter in a country with an elected government. Secondly, $N$ must himself have a certain familiarity with those institutions. His act must be a participation in the political life of the country, which presupposes that he must be aware of the symbolic relation between what he is doing now and the government which comes into power after the election. The force of this condition becomes more apparent in relation to cases where 'democratic institutions' have been imposed by alien administrators on societies to which such ways of conducting political life are foreign. The inhabitants of such a country may perhaps be cajoled into going through the motions of marking slips of paper and dropping them into boxes, but, if words are to retain any meaning, they cannot be said to be 'voting' unless they have some conception of the significance of what they are doing. This remains true even if the government which comes into power does so in fact as a result of the 'votes' cast.

## 3. *Activities and Precepts*

I have claimed that the analysis of meaningful behaviour must allot a central role to the notion of a rule; that all behaviour which is meaningful (therefore all specifically human behaviour) is *ipso facto* rule-governed. It may now be objected that this way of speaking blurs a necessary distinction: that *some* kinds of activity involve the participant in the observance of rules, whilst others do not. The free-thinking anarchist, for example, certainly does not live a life which is circumscribed by rules in the same sense as does the monk or the soldier; is it not wrong to subsume these very different modes of life under one fundamental category?

This objection certainly shows that we must exercise care in the use we make of the notion of a rule; but it does not show that the way of speaking which I have adopted is improper or unilluminating. It is important to notice that, in the sense in which I am speaking of rules, it is just as true to speak of the anarchist following rules in what he does as it is to say the same thing of the monk. The difference between these two kinds of men is not that the one follows rules and the other does not; it lies in the diverse *kinds* of rule which each respectively follows. The monk's life is circumscribed by rules of behaviour which are both explicit and tightly drawn: they leave as little room as possible for individual choice in situations which call for action. The anarchist, on the other hand, eschews explicit norms as far as possible and prides himself on considering all claims for action 'on their merits': that is, his choice is not determined in advance for him by the rule he is following. But that does not mean that we can eliminate altogether the idea of a rule from the description of his behaviour.

We cannot do this because, if I may be permitted a significant pleonasm, the anarchist's way of life is a *way of life*. It is to be distinguished, for instance, from the pointless behaviour of a berserk lunatic. The anarchist has reasons for acting as he does; he *makes a point* of not being governed by explicit, rigid norms. Although he retains his freedom of choice, yet they are still significant choices that he makes: they are guided by considerations, and he may have good reasons for choosing one course rather than another. And these notions, which are essential in describing the anarchist's mode of behaviour, presuppose the notion of a rule.

An analogy may help here. In learning to write English there are a number of fairly cut-and-dried grammatical rules which one acquires, such as that it is wrong to follow a plural subject with a singular verb. These correspond roughly to the explicit norms governing monastic life. In terms of correct grammar one does not have a choice between writing 'they were' and 'they was': if one can write grammatically the question of which of these expressions one should use just does not arise. But this is not the only kind of thing one learns; one also learns to follow certain stylistic canons, and these, while they guide the way in which one writes, do not *dictate* that one should write in one way rather than another. Hence people can have individual literary styles but, within certain limits, can write only correct grammar or incorrect grammar. But it would plainly be mistaken to conclude from this that literary style is not governed by any rules at all: it is something that can be learned, something that can be discussed, and the fact that it can be so learned and discussed is essential to our conception of it.

Perhaps the best way to support this point will be to consider a persuasive presentation of the case against it. Such a presentation is offered by Michael Oakeshott in a series of articles in the *Cambridge Journal*[1]. Much of Oakeshott's argument coincides with the view of human behaviour which has been presented here, and I will begin by considering this part of what he says before venturing some criticisms of the rest.

Very much in accordance with the view I have been advocating is Oakeshott's rejection of what he calls the 'rationalistic' misconception of the nature of human intelligence and rationality. (See 21.) According to this misconception the rationality of human behaviour comes to it from without: from intellectual functions which operate according to laws of their own and are, in principle, quite independent of the particular forms of activity to which they may nevertheless be applied.

A good example (not discussed by Oakeshott himself) of the sort of view to which he objects is Hume's famous assertion that 'Reason is, and ought only to be the slave of the passions, and can never pretend to any other office than to serve and obey them'. On this view the ends of human conduct are set by the natural constitution of men's emotions; those ends being given, the office of reason is mainly to determine the appropriate means of achieving them. The characteristic activities carried on in human societies spring then, presumably, from this interplay of reason and passion. Against this picture Oakeshott

[1]Reprinted in *Rationalism in Politics*, London, Methuen, 1962.

is quite correct to point out that: 'A cook is not a man who first has a vision of a pie and then tries to make it; he is a man skilled in cookery, and both his projects and his achievements spring from that skill'. (21.) Generally, both the ends sought and the means employed in human life, so far from generating forms of social activity, depend for their very being on those forms. A religious mystic, for instance, who says that his aim is union with God, can be understood only by someone who is acquainted with the religious tradition in the context of which this end is sought; a scientist who says that his aim is to split the atom can be understood only by someone who is familiar with modern physics.

This leads Oakeshott to say, again quite correctly, that a form of human activity can never be summed up in a set of explicit precepts. The activity 'goes beyond' the precepts. For instance, the precepts have to be applied in practice and, although we may formulate another, higher-order, set of precepts prescribing how the first set is to be applied, we cannot go further along this road without finding ourselves on the slippery slope pointed out by Lewis Carroll in his paper, justly celebrated amongst logicians, *What the Tortoise Said to Achilles* (5).

Achilles and the Tortoise are discussing three propositions, A, B, and Z, which are so related that Z follows logically from A and B. The Tortoise asks Achilles to treat him as if he accepted A and B as true but did not yet accept the truth of the hypothetical proposition (C) 'If A and B be true, Z must be true', and to force him, logically, to accept Z as true. Achilles begins by asking the Tortoise to accept C, which the Tortoise does; Achilles then writes in his notebook:

"A
B
C (If A and B are true, Z must be true)
Z."

He now says to the Tortoise: 'If you accept A and B and C, you must accept Z'. When the Tortoise asks why he must, Achilles replies: 'Because it follows *logically* from them. If A and B and C are true, Z *must* be true (D). You don't dispute *that*, I imagine?' The Tortoise agrees to accept D if Achilles will write it down. The following dialogue then ensues. Achilles says:

'Now that you accept A and B and C and D, *of course* you accept Z.'

'Do I?' said the Tortoise innocently. 'Let's make that quite clear. I accept A and B and C and D. Suppose I *still* refuse to accept Z?'

'Then Logic would take you by the throat, and *force* you to do it!' Achilles triumphantly replied. 'Logic would tell you "You can't help yourself. Now that you've accepted A and B and C and D, you *must* accept Z". So you've no choice, you see.'

'Whatever *Logic* is good enough to tell me is worth *writing down*,' said the Tortoise. ' So enter it in your book, please. We will call it

(E) If A and B and C and D are true, Z must be true. Until I've granted *that*, of course, I needn't grant Z. So it's quite a *necessary* step, you see?'

'I see,' said Achilles; and there was a touch of sadness in his tone.

The story ends some months later with the narrator

returning to the spot and finding the pair still sitting there. The notebook is nearly full.

The moral of this, if I may be boring enough to point it, is that the actual process of drawing an inference, which is after all at the heart of logic, is something which cannot be represented as a logical formula; that, moreover, a sufficient justification for inferring a conclusion from a set of premises is to see that the conclusion does in fact follow. To insist on any further justification is not to be extra cautious; it is to display a misunderstanding of what inference is. Learning to infer is not just a matter of being taught about explicit logical relations between propositions; it is learning *to do* something. Now the point which Oakeshott is making is really a generalization of this; where Carroll spoke only of logical inference, Oakeshott is making a similar point about human activities generally.

#### 4.  *Rules and Habits*

All the above fits in very well with the position outlined in Chapter I. Principles, precepts, definitions, formulae—all derive their sense from the context of human social activity in which they are applied. But Oakeshott wishes to take a further step. He thinks it follows from this that most human behaviour can be adequately described in terms of the notion of *habit* or *custom* and that neither the notion of a rule nor that of reflectiveness is essential to it. This seems to me a mistake for reasons which I shall now try to give.

In *The Tower of Babel* Oakeshott distinguishes

between two forms of morality: that which is 'a habit of affection and behaviour' and that which is 'the reflective application of a moral criterion' (20). He seems to think that that 'habitual' morality could exist in abstraction from 'reflective' morality. In habitual morality, he says, situations are met 'not by consciously applying to ourselves a rule of behaviour, nor by conduct recognized as the expression of a moral ideal, but by acting in accordance with a certain habit of behaviour'. These habits are not learned by precept but by 'living with people who habitually behave in a certain manner'. Oakeshott appears to think that the dividing line between behaviour which is habitual and that which is rule-governed depends on whether or not a rule is *consciously* applied.

In opposition to this I want to say that the test of whether a man's actions are the application of a rule is not whether he can *formulate* it but whether it makes sense to distinguish between a right and a wrong way of doing things in connection with what he does. Where that makes sense, then it must also make sense to say that he is applying a criterion in what he does even though he does not, and perhaps cannot, formulate that criterion.

Learning how to do something is not just copying what someone else does; it may start that way, but a teacher's estimate of his pupil's prowess will lie in the latter's ability to do things which he could precisely *not* simply have copied. Wittgenstein has described this situation very well. He asks us to consider someone being taught the series of natural numbers. Perhaps he has first to copy what his teacher has

written with his hand being guided. He will then be
asked to do the 'same' thing by himself.

> And here already there is a normal and an abnormal
> hearer's reaction ... We can imagine, e.g. that he does
> copy the figures independently, but not in the right order:
> he writes sometimes one sometimes another at random.
> And then communication stops at *that* point. Or again he
> makes '*mistakes*' in the order.—The difference between
> this and the first case will of course be one of frequency.—
> Or he makes a *systematic* mistake; for example he copies
> every other number, or he copies the series 0, 1, 2, 3, 4, 5
> ... like this: 1, 0, 3, 2, 5, 4 ... Here we shall almost be
> tempted to say he has understood *wrong*. (37: I, 143.)

The point here is that it *matters* that the pupil
should react to his teacher's example in one way
rather than another. He has to acquire not merely the
habit of following his teacher's example but also the
realization that some ways of following that example
are permissible and others are not. That is to say, he
has to acquire the ability to apply a criterion; he has
to learn not merely to do things in the same way as his
teacher, but also *what counts* as the same way.

The importance of this distinction may be brought
out by taking Wittgenstein's example a stage further.
Learning the series of natural numbers is not just
learning to copy down a finite series of figures in the
order which one has been shown. It involves *being able
to go on* writing down figures that have not been
shown one. In one sense, that is, it involves doing something *different* from what one was originally shown;
but *in relation to the rule* that is being followed, this
counts as 'going on in the *same* way' as one was shown.

There is a sense in which to acquire a habit is to

acquire a propensity to go on doing the same kind of
thing; there is another sense in which this is true of
learning a rule. These senses are different and a great
deal hangs on the difference. Let us consider the case
of an *animal* forming a habit: here there can be no
question of 'the reflective application of a criterion'.
Suppose that *N* teaches his dog to balance a lump of
sugar on its nose and to refrain from eating it until *N*
utters a word of command. The dog acquires a
propensity to respond in a certain way to *N*'s actions;
we have here a type of case which fits reasonably well
into the behaviourist's cherished category of stimulus
and response. *N*, however, being a simple dog-lover
rather than a scientist, no doubt speaks differently: he
says the dog has learned a trick. This way of speaking
is worth looking at, for it opens the door to the
possibility of assessing the dog's performance in
terms which do not belong to the stimulus-response
set of concepts at all. He can now say that the dog has
done the trick 'correctly' or 'incorrectly'. But it is
important to notice that this is an anthropomorphic
way of speaking; it requires a reference to *human*
activities, and norms which are here applied analogi-
cally to animals. It is only the dog's relation to human
beings which makes it intelligible to speak of his
having mastered a trick; what this way of speaking
amounts to could not be elucidated by any description,
however detailed, of canine behaviour in complete
isolation from human beings.

The same point is involved in pointing out that what
counts as 'always doing the same kind of thing when
the word of command is uttered' is decided by *N*
rather than by the dog. Indeed it would be nonsensical

to speak of the dog's doing this. It is only in relation to $N$'s purposes, involving as they do the notion of a trick, that the statement that the dog 'always does the same kind of thing' has any sense.

But whereas a dog's acquisition of a habit does not involve *it* in any understanding of what is meant by 'doing the same thing on the same kind of occasion', this is precisely what a human being has to understand before he can be said to have acquired a rule; and this too is involved in the acquisition of those forms of activity which Oakeshott wants to describe in terms of the notion of habit. A legal analogy may help here. Oakeshott's distinction between the two forms of morality is in many ways like the distinction between statute law and case law; and Roscoe Pound is taking up an attitude to this distinction somewhat analogous to Oakeshott's when he refers to statute law as 'the mechanical application of rules' and distinguishes it from case law which involves 'intuitions' (reminiscent of Oakeshott's discussion of politics in terms of 'intimations': see 22). This may sometimes be a helpful way of speaking, but it should not blind us to the fact that the interpretation of precedents, just as much as the application of statutes, involves following rules in the sense in which I have been using the expression here. As Otto Kahn-Freund puts it: 'One cannot dispense with a principle which links one decision with another, which raises the judicial act beyond the realm of sheer expediency'. (27; the reference to Pound is his *Introduction to the Philosophy of Law*, Chapter III. E. H. Levi gives an excellent concise account, with examples, of the way in which the interpretation of judicial precedents involves the application of rules: 14.)

It is only when a past precedent has to be applied to a new kind of case that the importance and nature of the rule become apparent. The court has to ask *what was involved* in the precedent decision and that is a question which makes no sense except in a context where the decision could sensibly be regarded as the application, however unselfconscious, of a rule. The same is true of other forms of human activity besides law, though elsewhere the rules may perhaps never be made so explicit. It is only because human actions exemplify rules that we can speak of past experience as relevant to our current behaviour. If it were merely a question of habits, then our current behaviour might certainly be *influenced* by the way in which we had acted in the past: but that would be just a causal influence. The dog responds to $N$'s commands now in a certain way because of what has happened to him in the past; if I am told to continue the series of natural numbers beyond 100, I continue in a certain way because of my past training. The phrase 'because of', however, is used differently of these two situations: the dog has been *conditioned* to respond in a certain way, whereas I *know* the right way to go on *on the basis of* what I have been taught.


## 5.   *Reflectiveness*

Many of the statements Oakeshott makes about habitual modes of behaviour sound like the things I have been saying about rule-governed behaviour.

Custom is always adaptable and susceptible to the *nuance* of the situation. This may appear a paradoxical assertion; custom, we have been taught, is blind. It is, however, an insidious piece of misobservation; custom is not blind, it is only 'blind as a bat'. And anyone who has studied a tradition of customary behaviour (or a tradition of any other sort) knows that both rigidity and instability are foreign to its character. And secondly, this form of the moral life is capable of change as well as of local variation. Indeed, no traditional way of behaviour, no traditional skill, ever remains fixed; its history is one of continuous change. (20.)

Nevertheless, the issue between us is not a merely verbal one. Whereas Oakeshott maintains that the sort of change and adaptability of which he here speaks occurs independently of any reflective principles, I want to say that *the possibility* of reflection is essential to that kind of adaptability. Without this possibility we are dealing not with meaningful behaviour but with something which is either mere response to stimuli or the manifestation of a habit which is really blind. I do not mean by this that meaningful behaviour is simply a putting into effect of pre-existing reflective principles; such principles arise in the course of conduct and are only intelligible in relation to the conduct out of which they arise. But equally, the nature of the conduct out of which they arise can only be grasped as an embodiment of those principles. The notion of a principle (or maxim) of conduct and the notion of meaningful action are *interwoven*, in much the same way as Wittgenstein spoke of the notion of a rule and the notion of 'the same' being interwoven.

To see this, let us look at one of the things Oakeshott says about the contrast between his alleged two forms of morality. He says that dilemmas of the form 'What ought I to do here?' are likely to arise only for someone who is self-consciously trying to follow explicitly formulated rules, not for someone who is unreflectively following an habitual mode of behaviour. Now it may well be true that, as Oakeshott alleges, the necessity for such heartsearchings is likely to be more frequent and pressing for someone who is trying to follow an explicit rule without a foundation of everyday experience in its application. But questions of interpretation and consistency, that is, matters for *reflection*, are bound to arise for anyone who has to deal with a situation foreign to his previous experience. In a rapidly changing social environment such problems will arise frequently, not just because traditional customary modes of behaviour have broken down, but because of the novelty of the situations in which those modes of behaviour have to be carried on. Of course, the resulting strain may *lead* to a breakdown in the traditions.

Oakeshott says that the predicament of Western morals is that 'our moral life has come to be dominated by the pursuit of ideals, a dominance ruinous to a settled mode of behaviour'. (20.) But what is ruinous to a settled mode of behaviour, of whatever kind, is an unstable environment. The only mode of life which can undergo a meaningful development in response to environmental changes is one which contains within itself the means of assessing the significance of the behaviour which it prescribes. Habits too may of course change in response to changing conditions. But human history is not just an account of changing habits: it is the story of how men have tried to carry over what they regard as important in their modes of behaviour into the new situations which they have had to face.

Oakeshott's attitude to reflectiveness is, as a matter of fact, incompatible with a very important point which he makes early on in the discussion. He says that the moral life is 'conduct to which there is an alternative'. Now though it is true that this 'alternative' need not be consciously before the agent's mind it must be something which *could* be brought before his mind. This condition is fulfilled only if the agent could defend what he has done against the allegation that he ought to have done something different. Or at least he must be able to *understand* what it would have been like to act differently. The dog who balances sugar on its nose in response to its master's command has no conception of what it would be to respond differently (because it has no *conception* of what it is doing at all). Hence it has no alternative to what it does; it just responds to the appropriate stimulus. An honest man may refrain from stealing money, though he could do so easily and needs it badly; the thought of acting otherwise need never occur to him. Nevertheless, he has the alternative of acting differently because he understands the situation he is in and the nature of what he is doing (or refraining from doing). Understanding something involves understanding the contradictory too: I understand what it is to act honestly just so far as and no farther than I understand what it is not to act honestly. That is why conduct which is the product of understanding, and only that, is conduct to which there is an alternative.

# CHAPTER THREE

# THE SOCIAL STUDIES AS SCIENCE

### 1. *J. S. Mill's 'Logic of the Moral Sciences'*

I TRIED to show in the last chapter how the view of philosophy presented in Chapter I leads to the discussion of the nature of human activities in society. I want next to consider some of the difficulties which arise if we try to base our understanding of societies on the methods of natural science. I start with John Stuart Mill for two reasons: first, because Mill states naively a position which underlies the pronouncements of a large proportion of contemporary social scientists, even if they do not always make it explicit; second, because some rather more sophisticated interpretations of the social studies as science, which I shall examine subsequently, can be best understood as attempts to remedy some of the more obvious defects in Mill's position. (Though I do not want to suggest that this represents the actual historical genesis of such ideas.)

Mill, like many of our own contemporaries, regarded the state of the 'moral sciences' as a 'blot on the face of science'. The way to remove this was to generalize the methods used in those subjects 'on which the results obtained have finally received the unanimous assent of all who have attended the proof'. (18: Book VI, Chapter I.) For this reason he regarded the philosophy of the social studies as just a branch of the philosophy of science. 'The methods of investigation applicable to moral and social science must have been already described, if I have succeeded in enumerating and characterizing those of science in general.' (*Ibid.*) This implies that, despite the title of Book VI of the *System of Logic*, Mill does not really believe that there is a 'logic of the moral sciences'. The logic is the same as that of any other science and all that has to be done is to elucidate certain difficulties arising in its application to the peculiar subject-matter studied in the moral sciences.

That is the task to which the main part of Mill's discussion is addressed. I want here to examine rather the validity of the thesis which his discussion takes for granted. To understand it we need to refer to Mill's conception of scientific investigation generally, which is based on Hume's ideas about the nature of causation. (See 12: Sections IV to VII; and 18: Book II.) To say that A is the cause of B is not to assert the existence of any intelligible (or mysterious) nexus between A and B, but to say that the temporal succession of A and B is an instance of a generalization to the effect that events like A are always found in our experience to be followed by events like B.

If scientific investigation consists in establishing causal sequences, then it seems to follow that we may have a scientific investigation of any subject-matter about which it is possible to establish generalizations. Indeed, Mill goes further: 'Any facts are fitted, in themselves, to be a subject of science, which follow

one another according to constant laws; although these
laws may not have been discovered, nor even be
discoverable by our existing resources'. (18: Book VI,
Chapter III.) That is, there may be science wherever
there are uniformities; and there may be uniformities
even where we have not yet discovered them and are
not in a position to discover them and formulate them
in generalizations.

Mill cites the contemporary state of meteorology as
an example: everybody knows that changes in atmo-
spheric conditions are subject to regularities; they are
therefore a proper subject for scientific study. This
has not got very far owing to 'the difficulty of observing the facts on which the phenomena depend'. The
theory of the tides ('Tidology') is in somewhat better
shape in that scientists have discovered the phenomena
on which the movements of the tides depend in
general; but they are unable to predict exactly what
will happen in particular circumstances owing to
the complexity of local conditions in the context
of which the gravitational effects of the moon
operate. (*Ibid.*)

Mill supposes that the 'science of human nature'
could at least be developed to the level of Tidology.
Owing to the complexity of the variables we may be
unable to do more than make statistical generalizations
about the probable outcome of social situations.
'The agencies which determine human character are
so numerous and diversified . . . that in the aggregate
they are never in two cases exactly similar.' Nevertheless,

> an approximate generalization is, in social inquiries, for
> most practical purposes equivalent to an exact one; that

which is only probable when asserted of individual human beings indiscriminately selected, being certain when affirmed of the character and collective conduct of masses.

*(Ibid.)*

Just as the irregularity of the tides as between different places on the globe does not mean that there are no regular laws governing them, so in the case of human behaviour. Individual divergences are to be explained by the operation of laws on highly diversified individual situations. So broad statistical generalizations are not ultimately enough: they must be 'connected deductively with the laws of nature from which they result'. These ultimate laws of nature are the 'Laws of Mind' discussed in Chapter IV of the *Logic;* they differ from 'empirical laws' not in kind but in their much greater degree of generality and exactitude. Like all scientific laws they are statements of uniformities, namely 'uniformities of succession among states of mind'. Mill raises the question whether these should be resolved into uniformities of succession between physiological states and states of mind and concludes that, though this may one day be possible to a significant degree, it does not vitiate the possibility of establishing autonomous psychological laws which do not depend on physiology.

'Ethology, or the Science of the Development of Character' can be based on our knowledge of the Laws of Mind. (18: Book VI, Chapter IV.) This comprises the study of human mental development, which Mill conceives as resulting from the operation of the general Laws of Mind on the individual circumstances of particular human beings. Hence he regards Ethology as 'altogether deductive', as opposed to

Psychology which is observational and experimental.

> The laws of the formation of character are . . . derivative
> laws, resulting from the general laws of mind, and are to
> be obtained by deducing them from those general laws by
> supposing any given set of circumstances, and then con-
> sidering what, according to the laws of mind, will be the
> influence of those circumstances on the formation of
> character. (*Ibid.*)

Ethology is related to Psychology as is mechanics to
theoretical physics; its principles are '*axiomata media*',
on the one hand derived from the general Laws of
Mind and on the other hand leading to the 'empirical
laws resulting from simple observation'.

The discovery of these lowest-level empirical laws is
the task of the historian. The social scientist aims to
explain the empirical laws of history by showing how
they follow, first from the *axiomata media* of Ethology,
and ultimately from the general laws of Psychology.
This leads Mill to his conception of the 'Inverse
Deductive Method'. Historical circumstances are so
exceedingly complex, owing to the cumulative effect
of 'the influence exercised over each generation by the
generations which preceded it' (18: Book VI, Chapter
X), that nobody could hope to achieve a sufficiently
detailed knowledge of any particular historical
situation to predict its outcome. So, in dealing with
large-scale historical developments, the social scientist
must, for the most part, wait and see what happens,
formulate the results of his observations in 'Empirical
Laws of Society', and finally 'connect them with
the laws of human nature, by deductions showing
that such were the derivative laws naturally to be

expected as the consequences of those ultimate ones'. (*Ibid.*)

Karl Popper has indicated some of the misconceptions in this account of the social sciences. In particular he has criticized what he calls Mill's 'Psychologism': the doctrine that the development of one social situation out of another can ultimately be explained in terms of individual psychology. He has also shown the confusions involved in describing the findings of history as 'empirical *laws* of society', rather than as statements of *trends*. (See 25: Chapter 14; and 26: Section 27.) Here I want to concentrate on some of the other elements in Mill's view; I hope thus to be able to show that Mill's conception of the social studies is open to much more radical objections even than those which Popper has brought forward.

## 2. *Differences in Degree and Differences in Kind*

Mill regards all explanations as fundamentally of the same logical structure; and this view is the foundation of his belief that there can be no fundamental logical difference between the principles according to which we explain natural changes and those according to which we explain social changes. It is a necessary consequence of this that the methodological issues concerning the moral sciences should be seen as *empirical:* an attitude involving a wait-and-see attitude to the question of what can be achieved by the social sciences and, incidentally, ruling the philosopher out of the picture.

But the issue is not an empirical one at all: it is

*conceptual*. It is not a question of what empirical research may show to be the case, but of what philosophical analysis reveals about *what it makes sense to say*. I want to show that the notion of a human society involves a scheme of concepts which is logically incompatible with the kinds of explanation offered in the natural sciences.

Both the rhetorical strength and the logical weakness of Mill's position revolve round the phrase 'just very much more complicated'. It is true, so the line of thought runs, that human beings react differently to their environment from other creatures; but the difference is just one of complexity. So the uniformities, though more difficult to discover in the case of humans, certainly exist; and the generalizations which express them are on precisely the same logical footing as any other generalizations.

Now though human reactions are very much more complex than those of other beings, they are not *just* very much more complex. For what is, from one point of view, a change in the degree of complexity is, from another point of view, a difference in kind: the concepts which we apply to the more complex behaviour are logically different from those we apply to the less complex. This is an instance of something like the Hegelian 'Law of the Transformation of Quantity into Quality' which I mentioned in connection with Ayer in the first Chapter. Unfortunately, Hegel's account of this, as well as Engels's gloss on Hegel, commits a mistake closely analogous to Mill's, in failing to distinguish physical changes from conceptual changes. They include, as instances of one and the same principle, the sudden qualitative change of water into ice following on a series of uniform quantitative changes of temperature, and on the other hand the qualitative change from hirsuteness to baldness following on a series of uniform quantitative changes in the number of hairs. (See 1: Chapter II, Section 7. For a detailed application of the principle to a particular sociological problem see 27, *passim.*)

By how many degrees does one need to reduce the temperature of a bucket of water for it to freeze?— The answer to that has to be settled experimentally. How many grains of wheat does one have to add together before one has a heap?—This cannot be settled by experiment because the criteria by which we distinguish a heap from a non-heap are vague in comparison with those by which we distinguish water from ice: there is no sharp dividing line. Neither, as Acton mentions, is there any sharp dividing line between what is and what is not alive: but that does not make the difference between life and non-life 'merely one of degree'. Acton says that 'the point at which we draw the line is one that we have to choose, not one that the facts press upon us in unmistakable fashion'. But though there may be a choice in border-line cases, there is not in others: it is not for me or anyone else to *decide* whether I, as I write these words, am alive or not.

The reaction of a cat which is seriously hurt is 'very much more complex' than that of a tree which is being chopped down. But is it really intelligible to say it is only a difference in degree? We say the cat 'writhes' about. Suppose I describe his very complex movements in purely mechanical terms, using a set of space-time co-ordinates. This is, in a sense, a description of what is going on as much as is the statement that the cat is writhing in pain. But the one statement could not be substituted for the other. The statement which includes the concept of writhing says something which no statement of the other sort, however detailed, could approximate to. The concept of writhing belongs to a quite different framework from that of the concept of movement in terms of space-time co-ordinates; and it is the former rather than the latter which is appropriate to the conception of the cat as an animate creature. Anyone who thought that a study of the mechanics of the movement of animate creatures would throw light on the concept of animate life would be the victim of a conceptual misunderstanding.

Similar considerations apply to my earlier comparison between the reactions of a dog who is taught a trick and those of a man who is taught a rule of language. Certainly the latter are very much more complex, but what is more important is the logical difference between the concepts which are applicable. Whereas the man learns to understand the rule the dog just learns to react in a certain way. The difference between these concepts *follows but cannot be explained in terms of* the difference in the complexity of the reactions. As indicated in the earlier discussion, the concept of understanding is rooted in a social context in which the dog does not participate as does the man.

Some social scientists have acknowledged the difference in concept between our currently accepted descriptions and explanations of natural and of social processes respectively, but have argued that the social scientist need not adhere to this non-scientific

conceptual framework; that he is at liberty to frame
such concepts as are useful for the kind of investigation
he is conducting. I shall consider some of the fallacies
in this line of thought in the next chapter; but Mill
does not follow it. He takes for granted the scientific
legitimacy of describing human behaviour in terms
which are current in everyday discourse. The Laws of
Mind are high-level causal generalizations setting out
invariable sequences between 'Thoughts, Emotions,
Volitions, and Sensations'. (18: Book VI, Chapter IV.)
And his argument against Libertarianism in Chapter
II is couched in terms of such conventional categories
as 'character and disposition', 'motives', 'purposes',
'efforts', and so on. I have next then to discuss the
attempt to interpret explanations of behaviour in
such terms as based on generalizations of the causal
type.

### 3.  Motives and Causes

It will not do simply to dismiss Mill as antediluvian,
for his approach flourishes still at the present time, as
can be seen by studying the discussion of motives in
T. M. Newcomb's prominent textbook of social psychology. (19: Chapter II). Newcomb agrees with Mill
in regarding explanations of actions in terms of the
agent's motives as a species of causal explanation; but
differs from him in regarding motives as physiological,
rather than psychological, states. A motive is 'a state
of the organism in which bodily energy is mobilized
and selectively directed towards part of the environment'. Newcomb also speaks of 'drives': 'bodily states
felt as restlessness, which initiate tendencies to

activity'. Clearly a mechanical model is at work here: it is as if the actions of a man were like the behaviour of a watch, where the energy contained in the tensed spring is transmitted *via* the mechanism in such a way as to bring about the regular revolution of the hands.

Why does Newcomb abandon Mill's caution about admitting Comte's claim that explanation in terms of motives should be reducible to physiological explanations? Is it that the once problematic physiological states have now been identified? Not at all for, as Newcomb says, 'nothing akin to a motive has ever been seen by a psychologist'. No, the identification of motives with 'states of the organism' is the action of a drowning man clutching at a straw. Newcomb thinks himself forced to this conclusion by the unacceptability of the only alternatives he can envisage: *viz.* that 'motives are merely figments of the psychologist's imagination' or else that the motive ascribed to a sequence of behaviour is simply a synonym for that behaviour itself.

He also imagines that there is compelling, though necessarily circumstantial, positive evidence. 'First, a behaviour sequence may show varying degrees of strength, or intensity, while its direction remains more or less constant.' 'The only way to account for such facts is to assume that a motive corresponds to an actual state of the organism.' Newcomb weights the scales heavily in his own favour by relying largely on examples which involve obviously physiological drives like hunger, thirst and sex; and by appealing mainly to experiments with _animals_ (to whose behaviour the concept of a motive is not obviously appropriate), he ensures that only the physiological

SOCIAL STUDIES AS SCIENCE

aspects of those drives shall be taken into account. But would it be intelligent to try to explain how Romeo's love for Juliet enters into his behaviour in the same terms as we might want to apply to the rat whose sexual excitement makes him run across an electrically charged grid to reach his mate? Does not Shakespeare do this much better?

Moreover, unless and until the 'actual state of the organism' is actually identified and correlated with the appropriate mode of behaviour, this type of explanation is as vacuous as those which Newcomb rejects. And the facts which he adduces certainly do not constitute *evidence* for the desired conclusion; the most one can say is that if there were good independent reasons for regarding motives as bodily states, those facts would not be incompatible with such a view. This is particularly obvious in connection with the 'experimental evidence', to which Newcomb appeals, provided by Zeigarnik in 1927. In these experiments a set of people were each given a series of twenty tasks and were told that there was a strict (though unspecified) time-limit for each task. But each subject was in fact allowed to complete only half his allotted tasks, irrespective of the time he had taken, and was given to understand that his permitted time had expired. Subsequently it was found that the subjects were inclined to remember the nature of the uncompleted tasks more readily than the others and to manifest a desire to be allowed to finish them. Newcomb comments:

> Such evidence suggests that motivation involves a mobilization of energy earmarked, as it were, for achieving a specified goal. The experimental data do not provide final

'proof' for such a theory, but they are consistent with it and
are difficult to explain in any other way. (19: p. 117.)

Now this evidence only 'suggests' such a conclusion to
someone who is already predisposed to believe it; and
the necessity for any special explanation is not in fact
obvious. The behaviour noted by Zeigarnik is perfectly
intelligible in such terms as the following: that the
subjects' interest had been aroused and they were
irritated at not being allowed to finish something
which they had started. If that sounds insufficiently
scientific to anyone, he should ask himself just how
much is added to our understanding by Newcomb's
way of talking. There is in fact a very simple, but
nonetheless cogent, argument against the physiological
interpretation of motives. To discover the motives of
a puzzling action *is* to increase our understanding of
that action; that is what 'understanding' means as
applied to human behaviour. But this is something we
in fact discover without any significant knowledge
about people's physiological states; therefore our
accounts of their motives can have nothing to do with
their physiological states. It does not follow, as
Newcomb fears, that motive explanations are either
mere tautologies or are an appeal to figments of the
imagination. But before I try to give a positive
account of what they do involve, there are some
further misconceptions to be removed.

Mill, as we have seen, rejects the physiological
account of motives, but he still wants to make motive
explanations a species of causal explanation. The
conception he wishes to advocate, though he is not
very explicit, seems to be something like this.—A

motive is a specific mental occurrence (in a Cartesian sense of 'mental' implying that it belongs wholly to the realm of consciousness). A toothache, for instance, is mental in this sense, whereas the hole in the tooth which gives rise to the ache is physical. It makes sense to say that someone has a hole in his tooth, of which he is unaware, but not that that he has a toothache of which he is unaware: 'unfelt ache' is a self-contradictory expression. The issue between Mill and Newcomb can now be phrased as follows: whereas Newcomb wants to assimilate motives (toothaches) to states of the organism (holes in the teeth), Mill insists that these are different and argues that it has yet to be shown whether to every motive (toothache) there corresponds a specific kind of organic state (dental decay). But what we can do, Mill argues, is to study the causal relation between motives, considered as purely conscious events, and the actions to which they give rise. This involves careful observation of what specific mental occurrences are associated with what actions—just as we might discover that certain kinds of stoppage in a motor engine are associated with a blocked carburettor and certain others with a defective sparking plug.

Mill's account does fit moderately well certain kinds of fact which we can discover about ourselves. For instance, I might come to associate a certain kind of headache with an incipient attack of migraine; every time I experience that kind of headache I can then predict that, within an hour, I shall be lying in bed in great discomfort. But nobody would want to call my headache the *motive* for the migraine.—Neither, of course, should we as a matter of fact be justified in

calling the headache the *cause* of the migraine: but
this raises general difficulties about the validity of
Mill's account of scientific method which it would be
out of place to discuss here.

### 4.  *Motives, Dispositions and Reasons*

Gilbert Ryle argues, against the kind of account
advocated by Mill, that to speak of a person's motives
is not to speak of any events at all, either mental or
physical, but is to refer to his general dispositions to
act in the ways in question. 'To explain an act as done
from a certain motive is not analogous to saying that
the glass broke, because a stone hit it, but to the quite
different type of statement that the glass broke, when
the stone hit it, because the glass was brittle.' (29:
p. 87.) There are a number of objections to this. For
one thing, there seems to be a danger of reducing
motive explanations to the sort of vacuity feared by
Newcomb. (An analogous point is made by Peter
Geach; See 10: p. 5.) Again, Ryle's account runs into
difficulties where we assign a motive to an act which
is quite at variance with the agent's previously
experienced behaviour. There is no contradiction in
saying that someone who never before manifested any
signs of a jealous disposition has, on a given occasion,
acted from jealousy; indeed, it is precisely when
someone acts unexpectedly that the need for a motive
explanation is particularly apparent.

But for my present purposes it is more important to
notice that though Ryle's account is different from
Mill's in many respects, it is not nearly different

enough. A dispositional, just as much as a causal, statement, is based on generalizations from what has been observed to happen. But a statement about an agent's motives is not like that: it is better understood as analogous to a setting out of the agent's *reasons* for acting thus. Suppose that $N$, a university lecturer, says that he is going to cancel his next week's lectures because he intends to travel to London: here we have a statement of intention for which a reason is given. Now $N$ does not *infer* his intention of cancelling his lectures from his desire to go to London, as the imminent shattering of the glass might be inferred, either from the fact that someone had thrown a stone or from the brittleness of the glass. $N$ does not offer his reason as *evidence* for the soundness of his prediction about his future behaviour. (Cf. Wittgenstein; 37: I, 629 ff.) Rather, he is *justifying* his intention. His statement is not of the form: 'Such and such causal factors are present, therefore this will result'; nor yet of the form: 'I have such and such a disposition, which will result in my doing this'; it is of the form: 'In view of such and such considerations this will be a reasonable thing to do'.

This takes me back to the argument of Chapter II, Section 2, which provides a way of correcting Ryle's account of motives. Ryle says that a statement about someone's motives is to be understood as a 'law-like proposition' describing the agent's propensity to act in certain kinds of way on certain kinds of occasion. (29: p. 89.) But the 'law-like proposition' in terms of which $N$'s reasons must be understood concerns not $N$'s dispositions but the accepted standards of reasonable behaviour current in his society.

The terms 'reason' and 'motive' are not synonymous. It would, for instance, be absurd to describe most imputations of motives as 'justifications': to impute a motive is more often to condemn than it is to justify. To say, for example, that $N$ murdered his wife from jealousy is certainly not to say that he acted reasonably. But it is to say that his act was *intelligible* in terms of the modes of behaviour which are familiar in our society, and that it was governed by considerations appropriate to its context. These two aspects of the matter are interwoven: one can act 'from considerations' only where there are accepted standards of what is appropriate to appeal to. The behaviour of Chaucer's Troilus towards Cressida is intelligible only in the context of the conventions of courtly love. Understanding Troilus presupposes understanding those conventions, for it is from them that his acts derive their meaning.

I have noted how the relation between $N$'s intention and his reason for it differs from the relation between a prediction and the evidence offered in its support. But somebody who knows $N$ and his circumstances well and who is familiar with the type of consideration which he is prone to regard as important, may on the basis of this knowledge predict how he is likely to behave. '$N$ has a jealous temperament; if his emotions in that direction are aroused he is likely to become violent. I must be careful not to provoke him further.' Here I adduce $N$'s motives as part of the evidence for my prediction of his behaviour. But though this is possible, *given* that I already possess the concept of a motive, that concept is not in the first place learned as part of a technique for making predictions (unlike the

concept of a cause). Learning what a motive is belongs
to learning the standards governing life in the society
in which one lives; and that again belongs to the
process of learning to live as a social being.

## 5. *The Investigation of Regularities*

A follower of Mill might concede that explanations
of human behaviour must appeal not to causal
generalizations about the individual's reaction to his
environment but to our knowledge of the institutions
and ways of life which give his acts their meaning.
But he might argue that this does not damage the
fundamentals of Mill's thesis, since understanding
social institutions is still a matter of grasping empirical
generalizations which are logically on a footing with
those of natural science. For an institution is, after
all, a certain kind of uniformity, and a uniformity can
only be grasped in a generalization. I shall now
examine this argument.

A regularity or uniformity is the constant recurrence
of the same kind of event on the same kind of occasion;
hence statements of uniformities presuppose judgements of identity. But this takes us right back to the
argument of Chapter I, Section 8, according to which
criteria of identity are necessarily relative to some
rule: with the corollary that two events which count
as qualitatively similar from the point of view of one
rule would count as different from the point of view of
another. So to investigate the type of regularity
studied in a given kind of enquiry is to examine the
nature of the rule according to which judgements of

identity are made in that enquiry. Such judgements are intelligible only relatively to a given mode of human behaviour, governed by its own rules.[1] In a physical science the relevant rules are those governing the procedures of investigators in the science in question. For instance, someone with no understanding of the problems and procedures of nuclear physics would gain nothing from being present at an experiment like the Cockcroft-Walton bombardment of lithium by hydrogen; indeed even the description of what he saw in those terms would be unintelligible to him, since the term 'bombardment' does not carry the sense in the context of the nuclear physicists' activities that it carries elsewhere. To understand what was going on in this experiment he would have to learn the nature of what nuclear physicists do; and this would include learning the criteria according to which they make judgements of identity.

Those rules, like all others, rest on a social context of common activity. So to understand the activities of an individual scientific investigator we must take account of two sets of relations: first, his relation to the phenomena which he investigates; second, his relation to his fellow-scientists. Both of these are essential to the sense of saying that he is 'detecting regularities' or 'discovering uniformities'; but writers on scientific 'methodology' too often concentrate on

[1] Cf. Hume: *A Treatise of Human Nature*, Introduction—"'Tis evident, that all the sciences have a relation, greater or less, to human nature; and that however wide any of them may seem to run from it, they still return back by one passage or another." Hume's remark is a further reminder of the close relation between the subject of this monograph and one of the most persistent and dominant *motifs* in the history of modern philosophy.

the first and overlook the importance of the second. That they must belong to different types is evident from the following considerations.—The phenomena being investigated present themselves to the scientist as an *object* of study; he observes them and notices certain facts about them. But to say of a man that he does this presupposes that he already has a mode of communication in the use of which rules are already being observed. For to notice something is to identify relevant characteristics, which means that the noticer must have some *concept* of such characteristics; this is possible only if he is able to use some symbol according to a rule which makes it refer to those characteristics. So we come back to his relation to his fellow-scientists, in which context alone he can be spoken of as following such a rule. Hence the relation between *N* and his fellows, in virtue of which we say that *N* is following the same rule as they, cannot be simply a relation of observation: it cannot consist in the fact that *N* has noticed how his fellows behave and has decided to take that as a norm for his own behaviour. For this would presuppose that we could give some account of the notion of 'noticing how his fellows behave' *apart from* the relation between *N* and his fellows which we are trying to specify; and that, as has been shown, is untrue. To quote Rush Rhees: 'We see that we understand one another, without noticing whether our reactions tally or not. *Because* we agree in our reactions, it is possible for me to tell you something, and it is possible for you to teach me something'. (28.)

In the course of his investigation the scientist applies and develops the concepts germane to his particular field of study. This application and modification are 'influenced' both by the phenomena *to* which they are applied and also by the fellow-workers *in participation with* whom they are applied. But the two kinds of 'influence' are different. Whereas it is on the basis of his observation of the phenomena (in the course of his experiments) that he develops his concepts as he does, he is able to do this only in virtue of his participation in an established form of activity with his fellow-scientists. When I speak of 'participation' here I do not necessarily imply any direct physical conjunction or even any direct communication between fellow-participants. What is important is that they are all taking part in the same general kind of activity, which they have all *learned* in similar ways; that they are, therefore, *capable* of communicating with each other about what they are doing; that what any one of them is doing is in principle intelligible to the others.

### 6.   *Understanding Social Institutions*

Mill's view is that understanding a social institution consists in observing regularities in the behaviour of its participants and expressing these regularities in the form of generalizations. Now if the position of the sociological investigator (in a broad sense) can be regarded as comparable, in its main logical outlines, with that of the natural scientist, the following must be the case. The concepts and criteria according to which the sociologist judges that, in two situations, the same thing has happened, or the same action performed, must be understood *in relation to the rules governing sociological investigation*. But here we run against a difficulty; for whereas in the case of the natural scientist we have to deal with only one set of rules, namely those governing the scientist's investigation itself, here *what the sociologist is studying*, as well as his study of it, is a human activity and is therefore carried on according to rules. And it is these rules, rather than those which govern the sociologist's investigation, which specify what is to count as 'doing the same kind of thing' in relation to that kind of activity.

An example may make this clearer. Consider the parable of the Pharisee and the Publican (*Luke*, 18, 9). Was the Pharisee who said 'God, I thank Thee that I am not as other men are' doing the same kind of thing as the Publican who prayed 'God be merciful unto me a sinner'? To answer this one would have to start by considering what is involved in the idea of prayer; and that is a *religious* question. In other words, the appropriate criteria for deciding whether the actions of these two men were of the same kind or not belong to religion itself. Thus the sociologist of religion will be confronted with an answer to the question: Do these two acts belong to the same kind of activity?; and this answer is given according to criteria which are not taken from sociology, but from religion itself.

But if the judgements of identity—and hence the generalizations—of the sociologist of religion rest on criteria taken from religion, then his relation to the performers of religious activity cannot be just that of observer to observed. It must rather be analogous to the participation of the natural scientist with his fellow-workers in the activities of scientific investigation. Putting the point generally, even if it is legitimate to speak of one's understanding of a mode of social activity as consisting in a knowledge of regularities, the nature of this knowledge must be very different from the nature of knowledge of physical regularities. So it is quite mistaken in principle to compare the activity of a student of a form of social behaviour with that of, say, an engineer studying the workings of a machine; and one does not advance matters by saying, with Mill, that the machine in question is of course immensely more complicated than any physical machine. If we are going to compare the social student to an engineer, we shall do better to compare him to an apprentice engineer who is studying what engineering—that is, the activity of engineering—is all about. His understanding of social phenomena is more like the engineer's understanding of his colleagues' activities than it is like the engineer's understanding of the mechanical systems which he studies.

This point is reflected in such common-sense considerations as the following: that a historian or sociologist of religion must himself have some religious feeling if he is to make sense of the religious movement he is studying and understand the considerations which govern the lives of its participants. A historian of art must have some aesthetic sense if he is to understand the problems confronting the artists of his period; and without this he will have left out of his account precisely what would have made it a history of *art*, as opposed to a rather puzzling external account of certain motions which certain people have been perceived to go through.

I do not wish to maintain that we must stop at the unreflective kind of understanding of which I gave as an instance the engineer's understanding of the activities of his colleagues. But I do want to say that any more reflective understanding must necessarily presuppose, if it is to count as genuine understanding at all, the participant's unreflective understanding. And this in itself makes it misleading to compare it with the natural scientist's understanding of his scientific data. Similarly, although the reflective student of society, or of a particular mode of social life, may find it necessary to use concepts which are not taken from the forms of activity which he is investigating, but which are taken rather from the context of his own investigation, still these technical concepts of his will imply a previous understanding of those other concepts which belong to the activities under investigation.

For example, liquidity preference is a technical concept of economics: it is not generally used by business men in the conduct of their affairs but by the economist who wishes to *explain* the nature and consequences of certain kinds of business behaviour. But it is logically tied to concepts which do enter into business activity, for its use by the economist presupposes his understanding of what it is to conduct a business, which in turn involves an understanding of such business concepts as money, profit, cost, risk, etc. It is only the relation between his account and these concepts which makes it an account of economic activity as opposed, say, to a piece of theology.

Again, a psychoanalyst may explain a patient's neurotic behaviour in terms of factors unknown to the patient and of concepts which would be unintelligible to him. Let us suppose that the psychoanalyst's explanation refers to events in the patient's early childhood. Well, the description of those events will presuppose an understanding of the concepts in terms of which family life, for example, is carried on in our society; for these will have entered, however rudimentarily, into the relations between the child and his family. A psychoanalyst who wished to give an account of the aetiology of neuroses amongst, say, the Trobriand Islanders, could not just apply without further reflection the concepts developed by Freud for situations arising in our own society. He would have first to investigate such things as the idea of fatherhood amongst the islanders and take into account any relevant aspects in which their idea differed from that current in his own society. And it is almost inevitable that such an investigation would lead to some modification in the psychological theory appropriate for explaining neurotic behaviour in this new situation.

These considerations also provide some justification for the sort of historical scepticism which that underestimated philosopher, R. G. Collingwood, expresses in *The Idea of History*. (6: *passim*.) Although they need not be brought to the foreground where one is dealing with situations in one's own society or in societies with whose life one is reasonably .familiar, the practical implications become pressing where the object of study is a society which is culturally remote from that of the investigator. This accounts for the weight which the Idealists attached to concepts like 'empathy' and 'historical imagination' (which is not to deny that these concepts give rise to difficulties of their own). It is also connected with another characteristic doctrine of theirs: that the understanding of a human society is closely connected with the activities of the philosopher. I led up to that doctrine in the first two chapters and shall return to it in the last two.

## 7.   *Prediction in the Social Studies*

In my discussion of Oakeshott in the last chapter I noticed the importance of the fact that voluntary behaviour is behaviour to which there is an alternative. Since understanding something involves understanding its contradictory, someone who, with understanding, performs X must be capable of envisaging the possibility of doing not–X. This is not an empirical statement but a remark about what is involved in the concept of doing something with understanding. Consider now an observer, $O$, of $N$'s behaviour. If $O$ wants to predict how $N$ is going to act he must familiarize himself with the concepts in terms of which $N$ is viewing the situation; having done this he may, from his knowledge of $N$'s character, be able to predict with great confidence what decision $N$ is going to take. But the notions which $O$ uses to make his prediction are nonetheless compatible with $N$'s taking a different decision from that predicted for him. If this happens it does not necessarily follow that $O$ has made a mistake in his calculations; for the whole point about a decision is that a given set of 'calculations' may lead to any one of a set of different outcomes. This is quite different from predictions in the natural sciences, where a falsified prediction always implies some sort of mistake on the part of the predictor: false or inadequate data, faulty calculation, or defective theory.

The following may make that clearer. To understand the nature of the decision confronting *N*, *O* must be aware of the rules which provide the criteria specifying for *N* the relevant features of his situation. If one knows the rule which someone is following one can, in a large number of cases, predict what he will do in given circumstances. For instance, if *O* knows that *N* is following the rule: 'Start with 0 and add 2 till you reach 1,000', he can predict that, having written down 104, *N* will next write 106. But sometimes even if *O* knows with certainty the rule which *N* is following, he cannot predict with any certainty what *N* will do: where, namely, the question arises of *what is involved* in following that rule, e.g. in circumstances markedly different from any in which it has previously been applied. The rule here does not specify any determinate outcome to the situation, though it does limit the range of possible alternatives; it is made determinate for the future by the choice of one of these alternatives and the rejection of the others—until such time as it again becomes necessary to interpret the rule in the light of yet new conditions.

This may throw some light on what is involved in the idea of a developing historical tradition. As I remarked earlier, Mill thought of historical trends as analogous to scientific laws and Popper wished to modify that conception by pointing out that the statement of a trend, unlike that of a true law, involves a reference to a set of specific initial conditions. I now want to make a further modification: even given a specific set of initial conditions, one will still not be

able to predict any determinate outcome to a historical trend because the continuation or breaking off of
that trend involves human decisions which are not
determined by their antecedent conditions in the context of which the sense of calling them 'decisions' lies.

Two words of caution are necessary in connection
with my last remark. I am not denying that it is
sometimes possible to predict decisions; only that
their relation to the evidence on which they are based
is unlike that characteristic of scientific predictions.
And I am not falling into the trap of saying that
historical trends are consciously willed and intended
by their participants; the point is that such trends
are in part the *outcome* of intentions and decisions of
their participants.

The development of a historical tradition may
involve deliberation, argument, the canvassing of
rival interpretations, followed perhaps by the adoption
of some agreed compromise or the springing up of
rival schools. Consider, for instance, the relation
between the music of Haydn, Mozart and Beethoven;
or the rival schools of political thought which all
claim, with some show of reason, to be based on the
Marxist tradition. Think of the interplay between
orthodoxy and heresy in the development of religion;
or of the way in which the game of football was
revolutionized by the Rugby boy who picked up the
ball and ran. It would certainly not have been possible
to predict that revolution from knowledge of the
preceding state of the game any more than it would
have been possible to predict the philosophy of Hume
from the philosophies of his predecessors. It may help
here to recall Humphrey Lyttleton's rejoinder to

someone who asked him where Jazz was going: 'If I knew where Jazz was going I'd be there already'.

Maurice Cranston makes essentially the same point when he notices that to predict the writing of a piece of poetry or the making of a new invention would involve writing the poem or making the invention oneself. And if one has already done this oneself then it is impossible to predict that someone else will make up that poem or discover that invention. 'He could not predict it because he could not say it was going to happen before it happened.' (8: p. 166.)

It would be a mistake, though tempting, to regard this as a piece of trivial logic-chopping. One appears to be attempting an impossible task of *a priori* legislation against a purely empirical possibility. What in fact one is showing, however, is that the central concepts which belong to our understanding of social life are incompatible with concepts central to the activity of scientific prediction. When we speak of the possibility of scientific prediction of social developments of this sort, we literally do not understand what we are saying. We cannot understand it, because it has no sense.

CHAPTER FOUR

———◆———

# THE MIND AND SOCIETY

## 1. *Pareto: Logical and Non-Logical Conduct*

WHAT I tried to show in Chapter III was that the
conceptions according to which we normally
think of social events are logically incompatible with
the concepts belonging to scientific explanation. An
important part of the argument was that the former
conceptions enter into social life itself and not merely
into the observer's description of it. But there is a
powerful stream of thought which maintains that the
ideas of participants must be discounted as more
likely than not to be misguided and confusing. To this
stream belongs, for instance, the quotation from
Durkheim at the end of Chapter I. I propose now to
examine the attempt made by Vilfredo Pareto, in *The
Mind and Society*, a title in which Pareto's translator
has most admirably caught his main preoccupation, to
show empirically that the ideas which people have, in
behaving as they do, influence the nature and outcome
of their behaviour far less fundamentally than is
usually thought; and that, therefore, the sociologist
must develop his own concepts *de novo* and pay as
little attention as possible to the ideas of participants.
My examination is designed to bring out two main

points: first that Pareto mistakes what is essentially a philosophical issue for an empirical, scientific, one; second, that the conclusion of his argument is in fact false.

Pareto starts by considering what is involved in a scientific approach to sociology. His answer is, roughly, that it consists in using only concepts which have a strictly empirical reference, in subjecting one's theories always rigorously to the control of observation and experiment, and in ensuring that one's inferences always follow strict logic. This he calls the 'logico-experimental' approach. The sociologist's data are the actions of human beings living together, and from these Pareto singles out, as requiring special attention, that behaviour which expresses an intellectual content.

> Current in any given group of people are a number of propositions, descriptive, preceptive or otherwise ... Such propositions, combined by logical or pseudo-logical nexuses and amplified with factual narrations of various sorts, constitute theories, theologies, cosmogonies, systems of metaphysics, and so on. Viewed from the outside without regard to any intrinsic merit with which they may be credited by faith, all such propositions and theories are experimental facts, and as experimental facts we are here obliged to consider and examine them. (23: Section 7.)

We are here concerned with Pareto's views on how the propositions and theories which people embrace are related to their other behaviour. How, for instance, are the propositions of Christian theology related to the practice of Christian rites? Now Pareto rightly points out that this question is ambiguous. It may

mean: Do these theories really constitute good reasons for the actions they purport to justify? Or it may mean: Is people's behaviour really governed by the ideas they embrace in the way they would claim, or would they go on behaving like that even if they ceased to embrace such ideas? Pareto conceives it to be the function of a scientific 'logico-experimental' sociology to answer both these questions; for this purpose he introduces two important distinctions: (i) that between *logical and non-logical* action; (ii) that between *residues and derivations*.

(i) is designed to throw light on the question how far the theories people embrace really constitute good reasons for the actions they perform.

> There are actions that use means appropriate to ends and which logically link means with ends. There are other actions in which those traits are missing. The two sorts of conduct are very different according as they are considered under their objective or their subjective aspect. From the subjective point of view nearly all human actions belong to the logical class. In the eyes of the Greek mariner sacrifices to Poseidon and rowing with oars were equally logical means of navigation ... Suppose we apply the term *logical actions* to actions that logically conjoin means to ends not only from the standpoint of the subject performing them, but from the standpoint of other persons who have a more extensive knowledge— in other words, to actions that are logical both subjectively and objectively in the sense just explained. Other actions we shall call *non-logical* (by no means the same as 'illogical'). (23: Section 150.)

A logical action then is one that fulfils the following conditions: (a) it is thought of by the agent as having a result and is performed by him for the purpose of achieving that result; (b) it actually does tend to have the result which the agent envisages; (c) the agent has (what Pareto would regard as) good (i.e. 'logico-experimental') grounds for his belief; (d) the end sought must be one that is empirically identifiable. The diversity of these criteria means that an action can also be non-logical in a variety of different ways, of which the following are among the most important. It may be non-logical because the agent does not think to achieve any end by it at all; this seems to correspond to what Max Weber meant by actions that are *wertrational* as opposed to *zweckrational*. But Pareto thinks these are few and far between because, he says, 'human beings have a very conspicuous tendency to paint a varnish of logic over their conduct' (Section 154). (It is interesting and important that he is unable to conceive of any way in which an action may have even the appearance of being logical except in terms of the category of means and ends.) Again, an action may be non-logical because, although the agent performs it for the sake of an end, it either achieves some quite different end or none at all. This may be because, as Pareto puts it, the end envisaged is not in fact a real one at all but is 'imaginary', because 'located outside the field of observation and experience' (Section 151): he several times mentions the salvation of the soul as an example of an 'imaginary' end of this sort. Or it may be because, although the end envisaged is a perfectly real one, it is not gained in the way the agent thinks it is: to this class Pareto assigns both operations in magic (Section 160) and also 'certain measures (for example, wage-cutting) of business men (entrepreneurs) working under conditions of free competition' (Section 159).

Now the inclusion of all these different types of action (and many more besides) within a single category is obviously going to give rise to serious difficulties. I should like here to concentrate on one such difficulty: that of making any clear distinction between 'non-logical' and 'illogical' conduct. In the above quotation from Section 150 of *The Mind and Society* we saw that Pareto maintained that these are 'by no means the same'; and he is making the same point when he writes, much later, that 'a mistake in engineering is not a non-logical action' (Section 327). Nevertheless, Pareto holds that the mistake of an entrepreneur under free competition, who thinks that by cutting his employees' wages he will increase his own profits is a non-logical action. How does a mistake in engineering differ relevantly from that of the entrepreneur (whose idea, Pareto says, may no longer be a mistake in conditions of monopoly)? And is the entrepreneur's mistake really comparable at all to the performance of a magical rite? Surely it ought rather to be compared to a *mistake* in a magical rite. The entrepreneur's mistake is a particular act (of which there may, nevertheless, be a great many similar examples) within the *category* of business behaviour; but magical operations themselves *constitute* a category of behaviour. Magic, in a society in which it occurs, plays a peculiar role of its own and is conducted according to considerations of its own. The same is true of business activity; but it is not true of the kind of *misguided* business activity to which Pareto refers, for that can only be understood by reference to the aims and nature of business activity in general. On the other hand, to try to understand magic by reference to the aims and nature of scientific activity, as Pareto does, will necessarily be to *mis*understand it.

The distinction between a general category of action —a mode of social life—and a particular sort of act falling within such a category, is of central importance to the distinction between non-logical and illogical behaviour. An *il*logical act presumably involves a *mistake* in logic; but to call something *non*-logical should be to deny that criteria of logic apply to it at all. That is, it does not make sense to say of non-logical conduct that it is either logical or illogical, just as it does not make sense to say of something non-spatial (such as virtue) that it is either big or small. But Pareto does not follow through the implications of this. For instance, he tries to use the term 'non-logical' in a logically pejorative sense, which is like concluding from the fact that virtue is not big that it must be small. A large part of the trouble here arises from the fact that he has not seen the point around which the main argument of this monograph revolves: that criteria of logic are not a direct gift of God, but arise out of, and are only intelligible in the context of, ways of living or modes of social life. It follows that one cannot apply criteria of logic to modes of social life as such. For instance, science is one such mode and religion is another; and each has criteria of intelligibility peculiar to itself. So within science or religion actions can be logical or illogical: in science, for example, it would be illogical to refuse to be bound by the results of a properly carried out experiment; in religion it would be illogical to suppose that one could pit one's own strength against God's; and so on. But we cannot sensibly say that either the practice of science itself or that of religion is either illogical or logical; both are non-logical. (This is, of course, an over-simplification, in that it does not allow for the overlapping character of different modes of social life. Somebody might, for instance, have religious reasons for devoting his life to science. But I do not think that this affects the substance of what I want to say, though it would make its precise expression in detail more complicated.) Now what Pareto tries to say is that science itself is a form of logical behaviour (in fact *the* form *par excellence* of such behaviour), whereas religion is non-logical (in a logically pejorative sense). And this, as I have tried to show, is not permissible.

There is a still deeper source for Pareto's failure to distinguish adequately between 'non-logical' and 'illogical'; it is connected with his belief that the appropriate way to produce a completely impartial, uncommitted theory of the workings of human societies is to be governed solely by 'logico-experimental' criteria, which he conceives on the analogy of what he takes to be the practice of the natural sciences. From this point of view he is clearly quite justified in evaluating rival theories *about* social existence (i.e. alternative *sociological* theories) by reference to those criteria. But he is constantly trying to do more than this: to evaluate by reference to the same criteria the ideas and theories which belong to the subject-matter he is studying. But this involves him in a fundamental confusion: that of taking sides in just the sort of way which the application of the logico-experimental

technique was supposed to preclude. The embarrass-
ment in which he is thus placed illustrates what I
wanted to emphasize in maintaining that the type of
problem with which he is here concerned belongs more
properly to philosophy than it does to science. This
has to do with the peculiar sense in which philosophy
is *uncommitted* enquiry. I noted in the first chapter how
philosophy is concerned with elucidating and comparing the ways in which the world is made intelligible
in different intellectual disciplines; and how this leads
on to the elucidation and comparison of different forms
of life. The uncommittedness of philosophy comes out
here in the fact that it is equally concerned to
elucidate its own account of things; the concern of
philosophy with its own being is thus not an unhealthy
Narcissistic aberration, but an essential part of what
it is trying to do. In performing this task the philosopher will in particular be alert to deflate the pretensions
of any form of enquiry to enshrine the essence of
intelligibility as such, to possess the key to reality.
For connected with the realization that intelligibility
takes many and varied forms is the realization that
reality has no key. But Pareto is committing just this
mistake: his way of discussing the distinction between
logical and non-logical conduct involves setting up
scientific intelligibility (or rather, his own misconception of it) as the norm for intelligibility in general;
he is claiming that science possesses the key to
reality.

Science, unlike philosophy, is wrapped up in its own
way of making things intelligible to the exclusion of
all others. Or rather it applies its criteria unself-
consciously; for to be self-conscious about such matters

*is* to be philosophical. This non-philosophical unself-consciousness is for the most part right and proper in the investigation of nature (except at such critical times as that gone through by Einstein prior to the formulation of the Special Theory of Relativity); but it is disastrous in the investigation of a human society, whose very nature is to consist in different and competing ways of life, each offering a different account of the intelligibility of things. To take an uncommitted view of such competing conceptions is peculiarly the task of philosophy; it is not its business to award prizes to science, religion, or anything else. It is not its business to advocate any *Weltanschauung* (in the way Pareto offers, inconsistently, a pseudo-scientific *Weltanschauung*). In Wittgenstein's words, 'Philosophy leaves everything as it was'.

In this connection it is worth while to recall Collingwood's allegation that some accounts of magical practices in primitive societies offered by 'scientific' anthropologists often mask 'a half-conscious conspiracy to bring into ridicule and contempt civilizations different from our own'. (7: Book I, Chapter IV.) A classic example of this corrupt use of 'scientific objectivity' is to be found in R. S. Lynd's *Knowledge for What?* (15: p. 121, footnote 7.) The philosophical confusions in Lynd's argument should be evident to anyone who has followed the argument of this monograph.

## 2. *Pareto: Residues and Derivations*

To develop this point further I now turn to the second of Pareto's distinctions: between *residues* and *derivations*. This distinction is supposed to perform two functions. In the first place it is supposed to provide *recurring* features in our observation of human societies, which will be a suitable subject for scientific generalization. Pareto argues that if one looks at a wide variety of different societies at different historical periods, one is struck by the fact that whereas certain kinds of conduct occur again and again with very little variation, other kinds are very unstable, changing constantly with time and differing considerably from one society to another. He calls the constant, recurring element 'residues'; they are what remains when the changeable features are left out of account. The variable elements are 'derivations', a term which refers to a fact about such kinds of conduct which Pareto claims to have discovered empirically: namely, that the main occupants of this category are the theories in terms of which people try to explain why they behave as they do. The derivation 'represents the work of the mind in accounting for [the residue]. That is why [it] is much more variable, as reflecting the play of the imagination'. (23: Section 850.) Because the derivations are so unstable and variable in comparison with the residues, Pareto urges, we must accept that the ideas and theories which people embrace have little real influence on the way they otherwise behave; embracing the theories cannot be a valid explanation of why people act in the given way, for that behaviour goes on even after the theories have been abandoned. The concept of a derivation obviously offers many points of comparison with, for example, the Marxian concept of an 'ideology' and the Freudian concept of a 'rationalization'. The

point I should like to emphasize here, however, is that
it is only by way of this conceptual distinction that
Pareto succeeds in finding common features of
different societies of a sort which appear suitable as a
subject for scientific generalization. That is, the
claim that there are sociological uniformities goes
hand in hand with the claim that human intelligence
is much overrated as a real influence on social
events.

I shall now quote an example of Pareto's detailed
application of the distinction.

> Christians have the custom of baptism. If one knew the
> Christian procedure only one would not know whether and
> how it could be analysed. Moreover, we have an explana-
> tion of it: we are told that the rite of baptism is celebrated
> in order to remove original sin. That still is not enough.
> If we had no other facts of the same class to go by, we
> should find it difficult to isolate the elements in the
> complex phenomenon of baptism. But we do have other
> facts of that type. The pagans too had lustral water, and
> they used it for purposes of purification. If we stopped at
> that we might associate the idea of water with the fact of
> purification. But other cases of baptism show that the use
> of water is not a constant element. Blood may be used for
> purification, and other substances as well. Nor is that all;
> there are numbers of rites that effect the same result . . .
> The given case, therefore, is made up of that constant
> element, *a*, and a variable element, *b*, the latter comprising
> the means that are used for restoring the individual's
> integrity and the reasonings by which the efficacy of the
> means is presumably explained. The human being has a
> vague feeling that water somehow cleanses moral as well
> as material pollution. However, he does not, as a rule,
> justify his conduct in that manner. The explanation would

be far too simple. So he goes looking for something more complicated, more pretentious, and readily finds what he is looking for. (23: Section 863.)

Now there are well-known philosophical difficulties which arise from the attempt to reject as nugatory whole classes of reasonings as opposed to particular appeals to that kind of reasoning within an accepted class. Consider, for instance, the often discussed difficulties involved in casting *general* doubt on the reliability of the senses, or of memory. But Pareto would no doubt maintain that his thesis is saved from this kind of vacuity by the mass of empirical evidence on which it rests. However, his thesis concerning the relative variability of derivations and constancy of residues is not, as he thinks, a straightforward report of the results of observation; it involves a conceptual misinterpretation of those results. The constant element, $a$, and the variable element, $b$, are not distinguished by observation but only as the result of an (illegitimate) abstraction. In the example quoted of the purification residues, the unvarying element is not just a straightforward set of physical movements for it may take a multitude of different physical forms (as Pareto himself is at pains to point out). The mere act of washing one's hands would not be an instance of it; it would become one only if performed with *symbolic* intent, as a sign of moral or religious purification. This point is so important that I will illustrate it with another example, the 'sex residues'. Pareto does not, as might be expected, mean to refer to the common factor of simple biological sexual intercourse which is found amidst all the multifarious social customs and moral ideas connected with sexual relations at different times and in different societies. He explicitly rules this out. To qualify as a residue a form of behaviour must have a quasi-intellectual, or symbolic content. 'Mere sexual appetite, though powerfully active in the human race, is no concern of ours here . . . We are interested in it only in so far as it influences theories, modes of thinking'. (23: Section 1,324.) For example, one dominant residue which Pareto discusses is the ascetic attitude to sexual relations: the idea that they are to be avoided as something evil or at least morally debilitating. But this constant factor, as in the previous example, is not something that Pareto has *observed* separately from the highly various moral and theological systems of ideas in terms of which sexual asceticism is justified or explained in different societies. It is something that he has analysed out of those systems of ideas by means of a conceptual analysis.

But ideas cannot be torn out of their context in that way; the relation between idea and context is an *internal* one. The idea gets its sense from the role it plays in the system. It is nonsensical to take several systems of ideas, find an element in each which can be expressed in the same verbal form, and then claim to have discovered an idea which is common to all the systems. This would be like observing that both the Aristotelian and Galilean systems of mechanics use a notion of force, and concluding that they therefore make use of the same notion. One can imagine the howl of rage which Pareto would send up at the philistinism of such a proceeding; but he is guilty of exactly the same kind of philistinism when, for instance, he compares the social relation between 'an

American millionaire and a plain American' to that between an Indian of high caste and one of low caste. (See Section 1,044.) And this sort of comparison is essential to his whole method of procedure.

The same point may be expressed as follows. Two things may be called 'the same' or 'different' only with reference to a set of criteria which lay down what is to be regarded as a relevant difference. When the 'things' in question are purely physical the criteria appealed to will of course be those of the observer. But when one is dealing with intellectual (or, indeed, any kind of social) 'things', that is not so. For their *being* intellectual or social, as opposed to physical, in character depends entirely on their belonging in a certain way to a system of ideas or mode of living. It is only by reference to the criteria governing that system of ideas or mode of life that they have any existence as intellectual or social events. It follows that if the sociological investigator wants to regard them *as* social events (as, *ex hypothesi*, he must), he has to take seriously the criteria which are applied for distinguishing 'different' kinds of actions and identifying the 'same' kinds of actions within the way of life he is studying. It is not open to him arbitrarily to impose his own standards from without. In so far as he does so, the events he is studying lose altogether their character as *social* events. A Christian would strenuously deny that the baptism rites of his faith were really the same in character as the acts of a pagan sprinkling lustral water or letting sacrificial blood. Pareto, in maintaining the contrary, is inadvertently removing from his subject-matter precisely that which gives them sociological interest: namely their internal connection with a way of living.

Miss G. E. M. Anscombe has remarked, in an unpublished paper, how there are certain activities— she mentions arithmetic as an example—which, unlike other activities, such as acrobatics, cannot be under-, stood by an observer unless he himself possesses the ability to perform the activities in question. She notes that any description of activities like arithmetic which is not based on arithmetical (or whatever) capacities is bound to seem pointless and arbitrary, and also compulsive in the sense that the steps no longer appear as meaningful choices. This is precisely the impression of social activities which is given by Pareto's account of them as residues; but the impression is not a well-founded one, it is an optical illusion based on a conceptual misunderstanding.

This shows, I think, that the whole presupposition of Pareto's procedure is absurd: namely that it is possible to treat propositions and theories as 'experimental facts' on a par with any other kind of such fact. (See 23: Section 7.) It is a presupposition which is certainly not peculiar to him: it is contained, for instance, in Emile Durkheim's first rule of sociological method: 'to consider social facts as things'. Pareto's statement, and the others like it, are absurd because they involve a contradiction: in so far as a set of phenomena is being looked at 'from the outside', 'as experimental facts', it cannot at the same time be described as constituting a 'theory' or set of 'propositions'. In a sense Pareto has not carried his empiricism far enough. For what the sociological observer has presented *to his senses* is not at all people holding certain theories, believing in certain propositions, but people making certain movements and sounds. Indeed, even describing them as 'people' really goes too far, which may explain the popularity of the sociological and social psychological jargon word 'organism': but organisms, as opposed to people, do not believe propositions or embrace theories. To describe what is observed by the sociologist in terms of notions like 'proposition' and 'theory' is already to have taken the decision to apply a set of concepts incompatible with the 'external', 'experimental' point of view. To refuse to describe what is observed in such terms, on the other hand, involves not treating it as having *social* significance. It follows that the understanding of society cannot be observational and experimental in one widely accepted sense.

What I am saying needs qualification. I do not mean, of course, that it is impossible to take as a datum that a certain person, or group of people, holds a certain belief—say that the earth is flat—without subscribing to it oneself. And this is all Pareto thinks he is doing; but actually he is doing more than this. He is not just speaking of particular beliefs *within* a given mode of discourse, but of whole modes of discourse. What he misses is that a mode of discourse has to be *understood* before anyone can speak of theories and propositions within it which could constitute data for him. He does not really consider the fundamental problem of what it is to understand a mode of discourse. In so far as he thinks anything about it he regards it as simply a matter of establishing generalizations on the basis of observation; a view which was disposed of in Chapter III.

There is, unfortunately, no space available to discuss further examples of attempts, like Pareto's, to eliminate human ideas and intelligence from the sociologist's account of social life. But readers may find it instructive to re-read Durkheim's *Suicide* in the light of what I have been saying. It is particularly important to notice the connection between Durkheim's conclusion —that conscious deliberations may be treated as 'purely formal, with no object but confirmation of a resolve previously formed for reasons unknown to consciousness', and his initial decision to define the word 'suicide' for the purposes of his study in a sense different from that which it bore within the societies which he was studying. (9.)

## 3. *Max Weber:* Verstehen *and Causal Explanation*

It is Max Weber who has said most about the peculiar sense which the word 'understand' bears when applied to modes of social life. I have already referred to his account of meaningful behaviour and propose in the next two sections to say something about his conception of sociological understanding (*Verstehen*). (See 33: Chapter 1.) The first issue on which I mean to concentrate is Weber's account of the relation between acquiring an 'interpretative understanding' (*deutend verstehen*) of the meaning (*Sinn*) of a piece of behaviour and providing a causal explanation (*kausal erklären*) of what brought the behaviour in question about and what its consequences are.

Now Weber never gives a clear account of the

*logical* character of interpretative understanding. He speaks of it much of the time as if it were simply a psychological technique: a matter of putting oneself in the other fellow's position. This has led many writers to allege that Weber confuses what is simply a technique for framing hypotheses with the logical character of the evidence for such hypotheses. Thus Popper argues that although we may use our knowledge of our own mental processes in order to frame hypotheses about the similar processes of other people, 'these hypotheses must be tested, they must be submitted to the method of selection by elimination. (By their intuition, some people are prevented from even imagining that anybody can possibly dislike chocolate).' (26: Section 29.)

Nevertheless, however applicable such criticisms may be to Weber's vulgarizers, they cannot justly be used against his own views, for he is very insistent that mere 'intuition' is not enough and must be tested by careful observation. However, what I think can be said against Weber is that he gives a wrong account of the process of checking the validity of suggested sociological interpretations. But the correction of Weber takes us farther away from, rather than closer to, the account which Popper, Ginsberg, and the many who think like them, would like to substitute.

Weber says:

Every interpretation aims at self-evidence or immediate plausibility (*Evidenz*). But an interpretation which makes the meaning of a piece of behaviour as self-evidently obvious as you like cannot claim *just* on that account to be the causally *valid* interpretation as well. In itself it is

nothing more than a particularly plausible hypothesis.
(33: Chapter I.)

He goes on to say that the appropriate way to verify
such an hypothesis is to establish statistical laws
based on observation of what happens. In this way he
arrives at the conception of a sociological law as 'a
statistical regularity which corresponds to an intelligible intended meaning'.

Weber is clearly right in pointing out that the
obvious interpretation need not be the right one.
R. S. Lynd's interpretation of West Indian voodoo
magic as 'a system of imputedly true and reliable
causal sequences' is a case in point (15: p. 121); and
there is a plethora of similar examples in Frazer's *The
Golden Bough*. But I want to question Weber's implied
suggestion that *Verstehen* is something which is
logically incomplete and needs supplementing by a
different method altogether, namely the collection of
statistics. Against this, I want to insist that if a
proffered interpretation is wrong, statistics, though
they may suggest that that is so, are not the decisive
and ultimate court of appeal for the validity of
sociological interpretations in the way Weber suggests.
What is then needed is a better interpretation, not
something different in kind. The compatibility of an
interpretation with the statistics does not prove its
validity. Someone who interprets a tribe's magical
rites as a form of misplaced scientific activity will not
be corrected by statistics about what members of that
tribe are likely to do on various kinds of occasion
(though this might form *part* of the argument); what
is ultimately required is a *philosophical* argument
like, e.g., Collingwood's in *The Principles of Art*. (6:

Book 1, Chapter IV.) For a mistaken interpretation of a form of social activity is closely akin to the type of mistake dealt with in philosophy.

Wittgenstein says somewhere that when we get into philosophical difficulties over the use of some of the concepts of our language, we are like savages confronted with something from an alien culture. I am simply indicating a corollary of this: that sociologists who misinterpret an alien culture are like philosophers getting into difficulties over the use of their own concepts. There will be differences of course. The philosopher's difficulty is usually with something with which he is perfectly familiar but which he is for the moment failing to see in its proper perspective. The sociologist's difficulty will often be over something with which he is not at all familiar; he may have no suitable perspective to apply. This may sometimes make his task more difficult than the philosopher's, and it may also sometimes make it easier. But the analogy between their problems should be plain.

Some of Wittgenstein's procedures in his philosophical elucidations reinforce this point. He is prone to draw our attention to certain features of our own concepts by comparing them with those of an imaginary society, in which our own familiar ways of thinking are subtly distorted. For instance, he asks us to suppose that such a society sold wood in the following way: They 'piled the timber in heaps of arbitrary, varying height and then sold it at a price proportionate to the area covered by the piles. And what if they even justified this with the words: "Of course, if you buy more timber, you must pay more"?'

(88: Chapter I, p. 142--151.) The important question for us is: in what circumstances could one say that one had *understood* this sort of behaviour? As I have indicated, Weber often speaks as if the ultimate test were our ability to formulate statistical laws which would enable us to *predict* with fair accuracy what people would be likely to do in given circumstances. In line with this is his attempt to define a 'social role' in terms of the probability (*Chance*) of actions of a certain sort being performed in given circumstances. But with Wittgenstein's example we might well be able to make predictions of great accuracy in this way and still not be able to claim any real understanding of what those people were doing. The difference is precisely analogous to that between being able to formulate statistical laws about the likely occurrences of words in a language and being able to understand what was being *said* by someone who spoke the language. The latter can never be reduced to the former; a man who understands Chinese is not a man who has a firm grasp of the statistical probabilities for the occurrence of the various words in the Chinese language. Indeed, he could have that without knowing that he was dealing with a language at all; and anyway, the knowledge that he was dealing with a language is not itself something that could be formulated statistically. 'Understanding', in situations like this, is grasping the *point* or *meaning* of what is being done or said. This is a notion far removed from the world of statistics and causal laws: it is closer to the realm of discourse and to the internal relations that link the parts of a realm of discourse. The notion of *meaning* should be carefully distinguished from that of *function*, in its quasi-causal sense, the use of which in social anthropology and sociology I shall not explore further here.


4.  *Max Weber: Meaningful Action and Social Action*

I can best bring out the implications of this by considering another aspect of Weber's view: his distinction between behaviour which is merely meaningful and that which is both meaningful and social. Now it is evident that any such distinction is incompatible with the argument of Chapter II of this book; all meaningful behaviour must be social, since it can be meaningful only if governed by rules, and rules presuppose a social setting. Weber clearly recognizes the importance of this issue for sociology even though he comes down on what I must regard as the wrong side. What is interesting is that in so doing he at the same time begins to write of social situations in a way which is quite incompatible with what he has said about *Verstehen;* this is just what one would expect in so far as *Verstehen* implies *Sinn* and *Sinn,* as I have argued, implies socially established rules. I am thinking here of the important paper: *R. Stammlers "Ueberwindung" der materialistischen Geschichtsauffassung* (34), where he connects together the following pair of assertions: first, that there is no *logical* difficulty in supposing a man to be capable of following rules of conduct in complete abstraction from any sort of social context; second, that there is no *logical* difference between the technique of manipulating natural objects (e.g. machinery) in order to achieve one's ends and that of 'manipulating' human beings as, he suggests, does the owner of a factory his employees. He says: 'that in the one case "events of consciousness" enter into the causal chain and in the other case not, makes "logically" not the slightest difference'; thus committing the mistake of supposing that 'events of consciousness' just happen to differ empirically from other kinds of event. He does not realize that the whole notion of an 'event' carries a different sense here, implying as it does a context of humanly followed rules which cannot be combined with a context of causal laws in this way without creating logical difficulties. Weber thus fails in his attempt to infer that the kind of 'law' which the sociologist may formulate to account for the behaviour of human beings is *logically* no different from a 'law' in natural science.

In trying to describe the situation he is using as an example in such a way as to support his point of view, Weber ceases to use the notions that would be appropriate to an interpretative understanding of the situation. Instead of speaking of the workers in his factory being paid and spending money, he speaks of their being handed pieces of metal, handing those pieces of metal to other people and receiving other objects from them; he does not speak of policemen protecting the workers' property, but of 'people with helmets' coming and giving back the workers the pieces of metal which other people have taken from them; and so on. In short, he adopts the external point of view and forgets to take account of the 'subjectively intended sense' of the behaviour he is talking about: and this, I want to say, is a natural result of his

attempt to divorce the *social relations* linking those
workers from the *ideas* which their actions embody:
ideas such as those of 'money', 'property', 'police',
'buying and selling', and so on. Their relations to each
other exist only through those ideas and similarly
those ideas exist only in their relations to each other.

I am not denying that it may sometimes be useful
to adopt devices like Weber's 'externalization' of his
description of this situation. It may serve the purpose
of drawing the reader's attention to aspects of the
situation which are so obvious and familiar that he
would otherwise miss them, in which case it is
comparable to Wittgenstein's use of imaginary
outlandish examples, to which I have already referred.
Again, it may be compared with the *Verfremdungseffekt* which Berthold Brecht aimed at in his theatrical
productions, or to Caradog Evans' use of outlandishly
literal translations from the Welsh in his sinisterly
satirical stories about West Wales.[1] The effect of all
these devices is to shake the reader or spectator out of
the complacent myopia which over-familiarity may
induce. What is dangerous is that the user of these
devices should come to think of *his* way of looking at
things as somehow more real than the usual way. One
suspects that Brecht may sometimes have adopted
this God-like attitude (as would be consistent with his
Marxism); it is certainly involved in Pareto's treatment
of 'residues'; and although it is an attitude which is on
the whole very uncharacteristic of Weber, it nevertheless follows very naturally from his methodological
account of the way in which social relations and

[1] This last example was suggested to me by conversations with my
colleague, Mr. D. L. Sims.

human ideas are related and from any attempt to compare sociological theories with those of natural science. The only legitimate use of such a *Verfremdungseffekt* is to *draw attention to* the familiar and obvious, not to show that it is *dispensable* from our understanding.

Moreover, if this mistake in Weber's account is corrected, it becomes much easier to defend his conception of *Verstehen* from a persistently reiterated criticism. Morris Ginsberg, for instance, writes:

> It appears to be a basic assumption of *verstehende Soziologie* and *verstehende Psychologie* that what we know within our minds is somehow more intelligible than what is outwardly observed. But this is to confuse the familiar with the intelligible. There is no inner sense establishing connexions between inner facts by direct intuition. Such connexions are in fact empirical generalizations, of no greater validity than the similar generalizations relating to outward facts. (11: p. 155.)

It must be said very firmly here that the case for saying that the understanding of society is logically different from the understanding of nature does not rest on the hypothesis of an 'inner sense' (a notion trenchantly criticized by Peter Geach.—10: Section 24.) In fact it follows from my argument in Chapter II that the concepts in terms of which we understand our *own* mental processes and behaviour have to be learned, and must, therefore, be *socially* established, just as much as the concepts in terms of which we come to understand the behaviour of other people. Thus Ginsberg's remark that the disgust induced by certain foods in someone who is subject to a taboo 'is not directly intelligible to anyone brought up in a different tradition', so far from being a valid criticism of the sort of view which I have tried to present of *Verstehen*, follows immediately from that view. I have already dealt, in Chapter III, with the idea that the connections embodied in our concepts of human behaviour are just the result of empirical generalizations.

# CHAPTER FIVE

# CONCEPTS AND ACTIONS

## 1. *The Internality of Social Relations*

TO illustrate what is meant by saying that the social relations between men and the ideas which men's actions embody are really the same thing considered from different points of view, I want now to consider the general nature of what happens when the ideas current in a society change: when new ideas come into the language and old ideas go out of it. In speaking of ' new ideas ' I shall make a distinction. Imagine a biochemist making certain observations and experiments as a result of which he discovers a new germ which is responsible for a certain disease. In one sense we might say that the name he gives to this new germ expresses a new idea, but I prefer to say in this context that he has made a discovery within the existing framework of ideas. I am assuming that the germ theory of disease is already well established in the scientific language he speaks. Now compare with this discovery the impact made by the first formulation of that theory, the first introduction of the concept of a germ into the language of medicine. This was a much more radically new departure, involving not merely a new factual discovery within an existing way of looking at things, but a completely new way of

121

looking at the whole problem of the causation of diseases, the adoption of new diagnostic techniques, the asking of new kinds of question about illnesses, and so on. In short it involved the adoption of new ways of doing things by people involved, in one way or another, in medical practice. An account of the way in which social relations in the medical profession had been influenced by this new concept would include an account of what that concept was. Conversely, the concept itself is unintelligible apart from its relation to medical practice. A doctor who (i) claimed to accept the germ theory of disease, (ii) claimed to aim at reducing the incidence of disease, and (iii) completely ignored the necessity for isolating infectious patients, would be behaving in a self-contradictory and unintelligible manner.

Again, imagine a society which has no concept of proper names, as we know them. People are known by general descriptive phrases, say, or by numbers. This would carry with it a great many other differences from our own social life as well. The whole structure of personal relationships would be affected. Consider the importance of numbers in prison or military life. Imagine how different it would be to fall in love with a girl known only by a number rather than by a name; and what the effect of that might be, for instance, on the poetry of love. The development of the use of proper names in such a society would certainly count as the introduction of a new idea, whereas the mere introduction of a *particular* new proper name, within the existing framework, would not.

I have wanted to show by these examples that a new way of talking sufficiently important to rank as a new

idea implies a new set of social relationships. Similarly
with the dying out of a way of speaking. Take the
notion of friendship: we read, in Penelope Hall's book,
*The Social Services of Modern England* (Routledge),
that it is the duty of a social worker to establish a
relationship of friendship with her clients; but that
she must never forget that her first duty is to the
policy of the agency by which she is employed. Now
that is a debasement of the notion of friendship as it
has been understood, which has excluded this sort of
divided loyalty, not to say double-dealing. To the
extent to which the old idea gives way to this new one
social relationships are impoverished (or, if anyone
objects to the interpolation of personal moral attitudes, at least they are *changed*). It will not do, either,
to say that the mere change in the meaning of a word
need not prevent people from having the relations to
each other they want to have; for this is to overlook
the fact that our language and our social relations are
just two different sides of the same coin. To give an
account of the meaning of a word is to describe how
it is used; and to describe how it is used is to describe
the social intercourse into which it enters.

If social relations between men exist only in and
through their ideas, then, since the relations between
ideas are internal relations, social relations must be a
species of internal relation too. This brings me into
conflict with a widely accepted principle of Hume's:
'There is no object, which implies the existence of any
other if we consider these objects in themselves, and
never look beyond the ideas which we form of them'.
There is no doubt that Hume intended this to apply to
human actions and social life as well as to the

phenomena of nature. Now to start with, Hume's principle is not unqualifiedly true even of our knowledge of natural phenomena. If I hear a sound and recognize it as a clap of thunder, I already commit myself to believing in the occurrence of a number of other events—e.g. electrical discharges in the atmosphere—even in calling what I have heard 'thunder'. That is, from 'the idea which I have formed' of what I heard I *can* legitimately infer 'the existence of other objects'. If I subsequently find that there was no electrical storm in the vicinity at the time I heard the sound I shall have to retract my claim that what I heard was thunder. To use a phrase of Gilbert Ryle's, the word 'thunder' is theory-impregnated; statements affirming the occurrence of thunder have logical connections with statements affirming the occurrence of other events. To say this, of course, is not to reintroduce any mysterious causal nexus *in rebus*, of a sort to which Hume could legitimately object. It is simply to point out that Hume overlooked the fact that 'the idea we form of an object' does not just consist of elements drawn from our observation of that object in isolation, but includes the idea of connections between it and other objects. (And one could scarcely form a conception of a language in which this was not so.)

Consider now a very simple paradigm case of a relation between actions in a human society: that between an act of command and an act of obedience to that command. A sergeant calls 'Eyes right!' and his men all turn their eyes to the right. Now, in describing the men's act in terms of the notion of obedience to a command, one is of course committing oneself to saying that a command has been issued. So far the situation looks precisely parallel to the relation between thunder and electrical storms. But now one needs to draw a distinction. An event's character as an act of obedience is *intrinsic* to it in a way which is not true of an event's character as a clap of thunder; and this is in general true of human acts as opposed to natural events. In the case of the latter, although human beings can think of the occurrences in question only in terms of the concepts they do in fact have of them, yet the events themselves have an existence independent of those concepts. There existed electrical storms and thunder long before there were human beings to form concepts of them or establish that there was any connection between them. But it does not make sense to suppose that human beings might have been issuing commands and obeying them before they came to form the concept of command and obedience. For their performance of such acts is itself the chief manifestation of their possession of those concepts. An act of obedience itself contains, as an essential element, a recognition of what went before as an order. But it would of course be senseless to suppose that a clap of thunder contained any recognition of what went before as an electrical storm; it is our recognition of the sound, rather than the sound itself, which contains that recognition of what went before.

Part of the opposition one feels to the idea that men can be related to each other through their actions in at all the same kind of way as propositions can be related to each other is probably due to an inadequate conception of what logical relations between propositions themselves are. One is inclined to think of the laws of logic as forming a *given* rigid structure to

which men try, with greater or less (but never complete) success, to make what they say in their actual
linguistic and social intercourse conform. One thinks
of propositions as something ethereal, which just
because of their ethereal, non-physical nature, can fit
together more tightly than can be conceived in the case
of anything so grossly material as flesh-and-blood
men and their actions. In a sense one is right in this;
for to treat of logical relations in a formal systematic
way is to think at a very high level of abstraction, at
which all the anomalies, imperfections and crudities
which characterize men's actual intercourse with each
other in society have been removed. But, like any
abstraction not recognized as such, this can be
misleading. It may make one forget that it is only from
their roots in this actual flesh-and-blood intercourse
that those formal systems draw such life as they have;
for the whole idea of a logical relation is only possible
by virtue of the sort of agreement between men and
their actions which is discussed by Wittgenstein in
the *Philosophical Investigations*. Collingwood's remark
on formal grammar is apposite: 'I likened the gram-
marian to a butcher; but if so, he is a butcher of a
curious kind. Travellers say that certain African
peoples will cut a steak from a living animal and cook
it for dinner, the animal being not much the worse.
This may serve to amend the original comparison'.
(7: p. 259.) It will seem less strange that social relations
should be like logical relations between propositions
once it is seen that logical relations between propositions themselves depend on social relations between
men.

What I have been saying conflicts, of course, with

Karl Popper's 'postulate of methodological individualism' and appears to commit the sin of what he calls 'methodological essentialism'. Popper maintains that the theories of the social sciences apply to theoretical constructions or models which are formulated by the investigator in order to explain certain experiences, a method which he explicitly compares to the construction of theoretical models in the natural sciences.

> This use of models explains and at the same time destroys the claims of methodological essentialism . . . It explains them, for the model is of an abstract or theoretical character, and we are liable to believe that we see it, either within or behind the changing observable events, as a kind of observable ghost or essence. And it destroys them because our task is to analyze our sociological models carefully in descriptive or nominalist terms, viz. *in terms of individuals*, their attitudes, expectations, relations, etc. —a postulate which may be called 'methodological individualism'. (26: Section 29.)

Popper's statement that social institutions are just explanatory models introduced by the social scientist for his own purposes is palpably untrue. The ways of thinking embodied in institutions govern the way the members of the societies studied by the social scientist behave. The idea of war, for instance, which is one of Popper's examples, was not simply invented by people who wanted to *explain* what happens when societies come into armed conflict. It is an idea which provides the criteria of what is appropriate in the behaviour of members of the conflicting societies. Because my country is at war there are certain things which I must and certain things which I must not do. My behaviour is governed, one could say, by my concept of myself as a member of a belligerent country. The concept of war belongs *essentially* to my behaviour. But the concept of gravity does not belong essentially to the behaviour of a falling apple in the same way: it belongs rather to the physicist's *explanation* of the apple's behaviour. To recognize this has, *pace* Popper, nothing to do with a belief in ghosts behind the phenomena. Further, it is impossible to go far in specifying the attitudes, expectations and relations of individuals without referring to concepts which enter into those attitudes, etc., and the meaning of which certainly cannot be explained in terms of the actions of any individual persons. (Cf. Maurice Mandelbaum: 17.)

## 2. *Discursive and Non-Discursive 'Ideas'*

In the course of this argument I have linked the assertion that social relations are internal with the assertion that men's mutual interaction 'embodies ideas', suggesting that social interaction can more profitably be compared to the exchange of ideas in a conversation than to the interaction of forces in a physical system. This may seem to put me in danger of over-intellectualizing social life, especially since the examples I have so far discussed have all been examples of behaviour which expresses *discursive* ideas, that is, ideas which also have a straightforward linguistic expression. It is because the use of language is so intimately, so inseparably, bound up with the other, non-linguistic, activities which men perform, that it is possible to speak of their non-linguistic behaviour also as expressing discursive ideas. Apart from the examples of this which I have already given in other connections, one needs only to recall the enormous extent to which the learning of any characteristically human activity normally involves talking as well: in connection, e.g., with discussions of alternative ways of doing things, the inculcation of standards of good work, the giving of reasons, and so on. But there is no sharp break between behaviour which expresses discursive ideas and that which does not; and that which does not is sufficiently like that which does to make it necessary to regard it as analogous to the other. So, even where it would be unnatural to say that a given kind of social relation expresses any ideas of a discursive nature, still it is closer to that general category than it is to that of the interaction of physical forces.

Collingwood provides a striking illustration of this in his discussion of the analogy between language and dress. (7: p. 244.) Again, consider the following scene from the film *Shane*. A lone horseman arrives at the isolated homestead of a small farmer on the American prairies who is suffering from the depredations of the rising class of big cattle-owners. Although they hardly exchange a word, a bond of sympathy springs up between the stranger and the homesteader. The stranger silently joins the other in uprooting, with great effort, the stump of a tree in the yard; in pausing for breath, they happen to catch each other's eye and smile shyly at each other. Now any explicit account that one tried to give of the kind of understanding that had sprung up between these two, and which was expressed in that glance, would no doubt be very complicated and inadequate. We understand

it, however, as we may understand the meaning of a
pregnant pause (consider what it is that makes a pause
*pregnant*), or as we may understand the meaning of a
gesture that completes a statement. 'There is a story
that Buddha once, at the climax of a philosophical
discussion . . . took a flower in his hand, and looked at
it; one of his disciples smiled, and the master said to
him, "You have understood me".' (7: p. 243.) And
what I want to insist on is that, just as in a conversation the point of a remark (or of a pause) depends on
its internal relation to what has gone before, so in the
scene from the film the interchange of glances derives
its full meaning from its internal relation to the situation in which it occurs: the loneliness, the threat of
danger, the sharing of a common life in difficult circumstances, the satisfaction in physical effort, and so on.

It may be thought that there are certain kinds of
social relation, particularly important for sociology
and history, of which the foregoing considerations are
not true: as for instance wars in which the issue
between the combatants is not even remotely of an
intellectual nature (as one might say, e.g., that the
crusades were), but purely a struggle for physical
survival  as in a war between hunger migrants and the
possessors of the land on which they are encroaching .[1]
But even here, although the issue is in a sense a purely
material one, the form which the struggle takes will
still involve internal relations in a sense which will
not apply to, say, a fight between two wild animals
over a piece of meat. For the belligerents are *societies*

---

[1] This example was suggested to me by a discussion with my colleague,
Professor J. C. Rees, as indeed was the realization for the necessity for
this whole section.

CONCEPTS AND ACTIONS        131

in which much goes on besides eating, seeking shelter and reproducing; in which life is carried on in terms of symbolic ideas which express certain attitudes as between man and man. These symbolic relationships, incidentally, will affect the character even of those basic 'biological' activities: one does not throw much light on the particular form which the latter may take in a given society by speaking of them in Malinowski's neo-Marxist terminology as performing the 'function' of providing for the satisfaction of the basic biological needs. Now of course, 'out-group attitudes' between the members of my hypothetical warring societies will not be the same as 'in-group attitudes' (if I may be forgiven the momentary lapse into the jargon of social psychology). Nevertheless, the fact that the enemies are *men*, with their own ideas and institutions, and with whom it would be possible to communicate, will affect the attitudes of members of the other society to them—even if its only effect is to make them the more ferocious. Human war, like all other human activities, is governed by conventions; and where one is dealing with conventions, one is dealing with internal relations.

### 3.   *The Social Sciences and History*

This view of the matter may make possible a new appreciation of Collingwood's conception of all human history as the history of thought. That is no doubt an exaggeration and the notion that the task of the historian is to re-think the thoughts of the historical participants is to some extent an intellectualistic distortion. But Collingwood is right if he is taken to mean that the way to understand events in human history, even those which cannot naturally be represented as conflicts between or developments of discursive ideas, is more closely analogous to the way in which we understand expressions of ideas than it is to the way we understand physical processes.

There is a certain respect, indeed, in which Collingwood pays insufficient attention to the manner in which a way of thinking and the historical situation to which it belongs form one indivisible whole. He says that the aim of the historian is to think the very same thoughts as were once thought, just as they were thought at the historical moment in question. (6: Part V.) But though extinct ways of thinking may, in a sense, be recaptured by the historian, the way in which the historian thinks them will be coloured by the fact that he has had to employ historiographical methods to recapture them. The medieval knight did not have to use those methods in order to view his lady in terms of the notions of courtly love: he just thought of her in those terms. Historical research may enable me to achieve some understanding of what was involved in this way of thinking, but that will not make it open to me to think of *my* lady in those terms. I should always be conscious that this was an anachronism, which means, of course, that I should not be thinking of her in just the same terms as did the knight of his lady. And naturally, it is even more impossible for me to think of *his* lady as he did.

Nevertheless, Collingwood's view is nearer the truth than is that most favoured in empiricist methodologies of the social sciences, which runs somewhat as follows —on the one side we have human history which is a

kind of repository of data. The historian unearths
these data and presents them to his more theoretically
minded colleagues who then produce scientific generalizations and theories establishing connections between
one kind of social situation and another. These
theories can then be applied to history itself in order
to enhance our understanding of the ways in which its
episodes are mutually connected. I have tried to show,
particularly in connection with Pareto, how this
involves minimizing the importance of ideas in human
history, since ideas and theories are constantly
developing and changing, and since each system of
ideas, its component elements being interrelated
internally, has to be understood in and for itself; the
combined result of which is to make systems of ideas
a very unsuitable subject for broad generalizations. I
have also tried to show that social relations really
exist only in and through the ideas which are current
in society; or alternatively, that social relations fall
into the same logical category as do relations between
ideas. It follows that social relations must be an
equally unsuitable subject for generalizations and
theories of the scientific sort to be formulated about
them. Historical explanation is not the application of
generalizations and theories to particular instances: it
is the tracing of internal relations. It is like applying
one's knowledge of a language in order to understand
a conversation rather than like applying one's
knowledge of the laws of mechanics to understand the
workings of a watch. Non-linguistic behaviour, for
example, has an 'idiom' in the same kind of way as
has a language. In the same kind of way as it can be
difficult to recapture the idiom of Greek thought in a

translation into modern English of a Platonic dialogue, so it can be misleading to think of the behaviour of people in remote societies in terms of the demeanour to which we are accustomed in our own society. Think of the uneasy feeling one often has about the authenticity of 'racy' historical evocations like those in some of Robert Graves's novels: this has nothing to do with doubts about a writer's accuracy in matters of external detail.

The relation between sociological theories and historical narrative is less like the relation between scientific laws and the reports of experiments or observations than it is like that between theories of logic and arguments in particular languages. Consider for instance the explanation of a chemical reaction in terms of a theory about molecular structure and valency: here the theory *establishes* a connection between what happened at one moment when the two chemicals were brought together and what happened at a subsequent moment. It is only *in terms of the theory* that one can speak of the events being thus 'connected' (as opposed to a simple spatio-temporal connection); the only way to grasp the connection is to learn the theory. But the application of a logical theory to a particular piece of reasoning is not like that. One does not have to know the theory in order to appreciate the connection between the steps of the argument; on the contrary, it is only in so far as one can already grasp logical connections between particular statements in particular languages that one is even in a position to understand what the logical theory is all about. (This is implied by the argument of Lewis Carroll, which I referred to earlier.) Whereas in natural science it is your theoretical knowledge which enables you to explain occurrences you have not previously met, a knowledge of logical theory on the other hand will not enable you to understand a piece of reasoning in an unknown language; you will have to learn that language, and that in itself *may* suffice to enable you to grasp the connections between the various parts of arguments in that language.

Consider now an example from sociology. Georg Simmel writes:

> The degeneration of a difference in convictions into hatred and fight occurs only when there were essential, original similarities between the parties. The (sociologically very significant) 'respect for the enemy' is usually absent where the hostility has arisen on the basis of previous solidarity. And where enough similarities continue to make confusions and blurred outlines possible, points of difference need an emphasis not justified by the issue but only by that danger of confusion. This was involved, for instance, in the case of Catholicism in Berne . . . Roman Catholicism does not have to fear any threat to its identity from external contact with a church so different as the Reformed Church, but quite from something as closely akin as Old-Catholicism. (31: Chapter I.)

Here I want to say that it is not *through* Simmel's generalization that one understands the relationship he is pointing to between Roman and Old Catholicism: one understands that only to the extent that one understands the two religious systems themselves and their historical relations. The 'sociological law' may be helpful in calling one's attention to features of historical situations which one might otherwise have overlooked and in suggesting useful analogies. Here for instance one may be led to compare Simmel's example with the relations between the Russian Communist Party and, on the one hand, the British Labour Party and, on the other, the British Conservatives. But no historical situation can be understood simply by 'applying' such laws, as one applies laws to particular occurrences in natural science. Indeed, it is only in so far as one has an *independent* historical grasp of situations like this one that one is able to understand what the law amounts to at all. That is not like having to know the kind of experiment on which a scientific theory is based before one can understand the theory, for there it makes no sense to speak of understanding the connections between the parts of the experiment except in terms of the scientific theory. But one could understand very well the nature of the relations between Roman Catholicism and Old Catholicism without ever having heard of Simmel's theory, or anything like it.

### 4. *Concluding Remark*

I have made no attempt, in this book, to consider the undoubted differences which exist between particular kinds of social study, such as sociology, political theory, economics, and so on. I have wanted rather to bring out certain features of the notion of a social study as such. I do not think that individual methodological differences, important as they may be within their own context, can affect the broad outlines of what I have tried to say. For this belongs to philosophy rather than to what is commonly understood by the term 'methodology'.

# BIBLIOGRAPHY

(1) ACTON, H. B., *The Illusion of the Epoch*, Cohen & West, 1955.

(2) ARON, RAYMOND, *German Sociology*, Heinemann, 1957.

(3) AYER, A. J., *The Problem of Knowledge*, Macmillan and Penguin Books, 1956.

(4) AYER, A. J., 'Can There be a Private Language?', *Proceedings of the Aristotelian Society*, Supplementary Volume XXVIII.

(5) CARROLL, LEWIS, 'What the Tortoise Said to Achilles', *Complete Works*, Nonesuch Press.

(6) COLLINGWOOD, R. G., *The Idea of History*, OUP, 1946.

(7) COLLINGWOOD, R. G., *The Principles of Art*, OUP, 1938.

(8) CRANSTON, MAURICE, *Freedom: A New Analysis*, Longmans, 1953.

(9) DURKHEIM, EMILE, *Suicide*, Routledge & Kegan Paul, 1952.

(10) GEACH, PETER, *Mental Acts*, Routledge & Kegan Paul, 1957.

(11) GINSBERG, MORRIS, *On the Diversity of Morals*, Heinemann, 1956.

(12) HUME, DAVID, *Enquiry into Human Understanding*.

(13) LASLETT, PETER (Ed.), *Philosophy, Politics and Society*, Blackwell, 1956.

(14) LEVI, E. H., *An Introduction to Legal Reasoning*, University of Chicago, Phoenix Books, 1961.

(15) LYND, R. S., *Knowledge for What?*, Princeton, 1945.

(16) MALCOLM, NORMAN, Article in the *Philosophical Review*, Vol. LXIII, 1954, pp. 530–559.

(17) MANDELBAUM, MAURICE, 'Societal Facts', *B. J. Sociol.*, VI, 4 (1955).

(18) MILL, J. S., *A System of Logic.*

(19) NEWCOMB, T. M., *Social Psychology*, Tavistock Publications, 1952.

(20) OAKESHOTT, Michael, 'The Tower of Babel', *Cambridge Journal*, Vol. 2.

(21) OAKESHOTT, MICHAEL, 'Rational Conduct', *Cambridge Journal*, Vol. 4.

(22) OAKESHOTT, MICHAEL, *Political Education*, Bowes and Bowes, 1951.

(23) PARETO, VILFREDO, *The Mind and Society*, New York, Harcourt Brace, 1935.

(24) PARSONS, TALCOTT, *The Structure of Social Action*, Allen & Unwin, 1949.

(25) POPPER, KARL, *The Open Society and Its Enemies*, Routledge & Kegan Paul, 1945.

(26) POPPER, KARL, *The Poverty of Historicism*, Routledge & Kegan Paul, 1957.

(27) RENNER, KARL (with Introduction by O. KAHN-FREUND), *The Institutions of Private Law and their Social Function*, Routledge & Kegan Paul, 1949.

(28) RHEES, RUSH, 'Can There be a Private Language?', *Proceedings of the Aristotelian Society*, Supplementary Volume XXVIII.

(29) RYLE, GILBERT, *The Concept of Mind*, Hutchinson, 1949.

(30) SHERIF, M. & SHERIF, C., *An Outline of Social Psychology*, New York, Harper, 1956.

(31) SIMMEL, GEORG, *Conflict*, Glencoe, Free Press, 1955.

(32) STRAWSON, P. F., Critical Notice in *Mind*, Vol. LXIII, No. 249, pp. 84 ff.

(33) WEBER, MAX, *Wirtschaft und Gesellschaft*, Tübingen, Mohr, 1956.

(34) WEBER, MAX, *Gesammelte Aufsätze zur Wissenschaftslehre*, Tübingen, Mohr, 1922.

(35) WELDON, T. D., *The Vocabulary of Politics*, Penguin Books, 1953.
(36) WITTGENSTEIN, LUDWIG, *Tractatus Logico-Philosophicus*, Kegan Paul, 1923.
(37) WITTGENSTEIN, LUDWIG, *Philosophical Investigations*, Blackwell, 1953.
(38) WITTGENSTEIN, LUDWIG, *Remarks on the Foundations of Mathematics*, Blackwell, 1956.

# INDEX